Robert Hart,
the first English-speaking
settler in South Africa

First publication 2018 by Footprints Press, South Africa

Website: www.hiltonbarber.co.za

Cover design and page layout by Anthony Cuerden
Email: ant@flyingant.co.za

Printed by Pinetown Printers (Pty) Ltd; Pinetown, KwaZulu-Natal

ISBN: 978-0-620-78469-6

Robert Hart,
the first English-speaking settler in South Africa

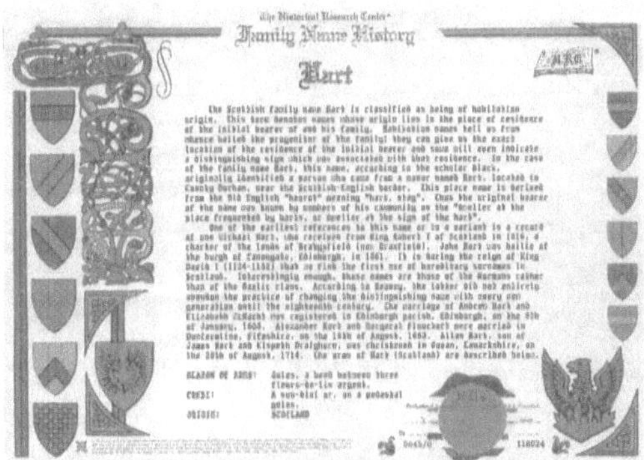

By David Hilton-Barber

'It is no more than the grateful duty of a succeeding

generation to revere the memory of those who bore the

heat and burden of the days long gone.

But better than merely holding in one's memories of

departed heroes is the placing on permanent record the

account of their lives and works'

George Cory, historian.

'The past no longer belongs only to those
who lived in it; the past belongs to those who
claim it, and are willing to explore it and
infuse it with meaning for those alive today.'

Margaret Atwood, novelist

Foreword

When I think of David Hilton-Barber's books I imagine them on the shelves of a 22nd Century antiquarian store many generations from now, with the printed word still as respected as the digital one.

I picture a young historian, travel writer or simply someone curious about how life was once lived in Southern Africa, strolling into this bookshop of the future and discovering Hilton-Barber's work with pure delight.

Whether he's telling you about the exploits (both infamous and glorious) of his ancestors or the other adventurers and scallywags who make up South Africa's historical palette, chances are you will be charmed. You will also be able to see the country more clearly in context.

His latest effort, *Robert Hart – The first English-speaking settler in South Africa*, takes you, the reader, from the Highlands of Scotland to the frontier lands of the Eastern Cape, then part of the Cape Colony.

Robert Hart is widely acknowledged as a pioneering soldier-farmer who was already well established in the Eastern Cape by the time 1820 and its 4 000 wide-eyed British settlers arrived.

He'd fought in the various defences of Grahamstown and then went on to run Somerset Farm, which supplied food and fodder to both the local military and the Pringle Party up in the Baviaans. Thomas Pringle had this to say about Hart:

"The friendship of this able and active man proved …of great advantage to our party."

In 1821, Hart was given the land where Glen Avon Farm now stands, not far from Somerset East. And although the family name has turned to Brown, seven generations of the same clan have worked this wonderful farm at the foot of the Boschberg.

Some would say it is high time Robert Hart was given his rightful place in the historical sun. David Hilton-Barber, who has four generations of 1820 Settler blood in his veins, is just the man for the job.

Chris Marais
Karoo Space

Acknowledgments

As a writer of South African non-fiction historical works, I was intrigue to be given an introduction to Oliver Hart, great grandson of Robert Hart, the subject of this book. At our first meeting in his home in Grahamstown, Oliver took me to his garage where he showed me a cabinet filled with box files. Without hesitation, he selected half a dozen for me to take away. There followed several months of fascinating exploration of this comprehensive collection of documents, letters, newspaper clippings, extracts from books and photographs. I am indebted to John Bond whose book, *They Were South Africans*, published over 60 years ago, provided valuable context.

Further research at the Cory Library at Rhodes University yielded more information. Finally I visited Glen Avon, Robert Hart's original farm in Somerset East, still owned by his descendants, where Greg Brown offered further insights into the narrative. This rounded off my task of presenting this historical work for those interested in the early history of the Eastern Cape.

Editor's note: The original spelling of such names as *Kafirland, cafir, caffers* etc has been retained.

Contents

Introduction

It has been truly said that Scotland's greatest export is Scotsmen (though the 'usquebaugh'- Gaelic word for whiskey; literally water of life must be a close second). There are 4.1 million people in Scotland, but there must be many times that number living abroad.[1]

In fact the running of the United Kingdom was not much of a challenge, so the Scots had to look for fresh fields for the exercise of their talents. From then on they spread to every corner of the globe. All over the world, if there was a colony to be established, a heathen to be Christianised, ignorant to be educated, land to be farmed, a road, a bridge or a railway to be built, a newspaper to be published, a bank to be established, insurance to be organised, a sick body to be healed, a mine to be sunk, a harbour to be constructed, a ship to be built or sailed, or a cargo to be bought and sold —then a Scot was there to do it.

One of the places in which their impact was most distinctly felt was the southern tip of the African continent. The first on the list must be Private Robert Hart, the first British person to land in the Cape and later to settle there. A good deal has been written about him, but what may not be generally known is that in later life he was not only a Grahamstown farmer (actually in what is now Somerset East) but also a contractor.

He played a key part in Afrikaner (Dutch) history by speeding the Voortrekkers on their way with a supply of wagons, oxen, firearms, brandy and various other necessities. He thus contributed indirectly (and no doubt profitably) to the opening up of the northern and eastern parts of South Africa.

The life of Robert Hart was contemporaneous with the whole history of the Cape Colony under British rule, and to write a complete history of his life would be to write, in a, great measure, a history of the colony. Had he kept a diary, it might not only have been interesting and instructive, but could have been taken as a text book to the history of the Colony, as he came to the Cape in the year 1795 with the British troops under Sir

1. Molly Reinhardt, *With Love and Hisses*, Sunday Times, 28 Feb 1971

Home Popham,[2] and was at the first taking of the Cape.

John Bond:[3] *The name of Robert Hart must be unknown to almost everyone who is listening to me tonight. That is strange, because Hart, as far as I can discover, was the first English-speaking South African. He was founder of that new race whose arrival in South Africa tipped the scale the right way when it wavered in the balance between civilisation and barbarism.*

Robert Hart would have asserted to that. He came to South Africa in its darkest period when the Dutch East India Company's rule was breaking down completely. His whole life, from the day he landed in 1795, was devoted one way or another to shoring up the shaky structure of the Cape.

That very crisis in the rise of our country was a result of the trekker's success, with precious little assistance from their rulers, in crossing the desert zone which had insulated the Cape from the Bantu for almost 140 years after Van Riebeeck.

---

2. Admiral Popham's first visit to the Cape was in 1793. However his ship was seized, partly on the grounds that he was carrying contraband, and partly because he was infringing the East India Company's monopoly

3. From the Series *They Were South Africans*, a broadcast on the English transmission by the journalist and historian, John Bond, published in the SABC magazine on 19 July 1954

A laager for defence at Zuurveld

The British Army charging the enemy at Zuurveld

Robert Hart bust by
Ivan Mitford-Barberton

1.

Who was Robert Hart?

Physically Robert Hart was described as of middle height with a wiry and muscular frame, and capable of the most intense labour. It is told of him that when he had passed his three score years and ten, he outran a whole field of natives in a mile, and within a few months of his death (at the age of ninety) he rode on horseback over the Boschberg.

Sir Gordon Sprigg, who married a grand-daughter, described him as a self-made man marked by a rugged independence.[4]

His character was noted for its mental and moral strength. Independent and self-reliant, he was decided and emphatic in his judgments and resolutions. There was nothing small about him. Meanness, dodges and subterfuges he abhorred and he was a man of absolute truth, whose word could always-be relied upon. He was open, just and trustworthy in all he did, and no bribe could buy him from the path of rectitude. He hated oppression and injustice and he spent time, energy and money in the moral and religious uplift of the native race. He did much to bring out missionaries and his advice on native needs and questions was acted upon by the Missionary authorities in the Old Country.[5]

He was emphatically self-reliant; he was not subject to doubt or hesitation; he believed in himself. He was very far removed from littleness; he had the utmost abhorrence and contempt for everything approaching meanness; he knew nothing of dodges; falsehood never passed his lips; he was clear and open as the daylight, a man of inflexible justice, a man

---

4. Sir Gordon Sprigg married a grand-daughter

5. His wife was a strict Calvinistic as evidenced in her removing some 'evil' brass statuettes from Burma which adorned an imported sideboard in the house, and having them buried in the river bank somewhere on the farm

eminently to be trusted. He was indeed of such a character that one was of times led to speculate whether any bait could be presented that would lure him from the path of moral rectitude. But though there was a noble severity in his bearing, yet it was relieved by a certain quaintness, a playful humour and a genial laugh which at once put a stranger at ease in his company.

His manners, too, especially in his later years, were marked by a great courtesy towards those who were but children beside him in age, but whom he regarded as having the advantages of a superior education; and one calls to mind as a pleasant reminiscence the 'sir' with which he was wont to commence or close his observations, and the great deference which he paid to anyone who communicated to him fresh information for although possessed of a great store of knowledge upon a variety of subjects he was to the last a willing learner. It is awarding him the highest praise to say to those to whom he was most intimately known he was held in the greatest respect.

Like the Arabian chieftain of sacred story, he has gone down to the grave full of days and full of honour, and with the parting of his aged form we feel that 'he was a man, take him for all in all, we ne'er shall look upon his like again.[6]

He was always keenly interested in the religious life of both Europeans and natives and he took a large part in the establishment of a leper settlement, and by his generosity helped to maintain it. The Lovedale Institution claimed and had his entire sympathy, shown by his assistance in money and in other ways.

People from all over the country came to Hart for help while he was at the Somerset Farm. One night in 1817 Mrs Hart was awakened by hearing a voice calling 'Hart, Hart'. Three times came the call but when Hart finally opened his front door no one was there. Next morning the owner of the voice, a native carrying a letter in a cleft stick, returned to the house. The letter was from Mrs Williams, the wife of the missionary,

____

6. Adaptation from a verse in *Hamlet*

Joseph Williams, at the Kat River. Her husband had died of a fever and Mrs Williams wrote that she and her children were alone at the mission with the Natives. Hart's typical response to this letter was to pack an ox wagon and, with Mrs Hart, set off immediately, for the Kat River. They found Mrs Williams digging her husband's grave by herself. The Harts brought the sad little family back to Somerset Farm where they remained for some weeks before proceeding to Cape Town.

Why was he known as the first South African?

Though he might appropriately have been styled an 'old inhabitant' by the time the 1820 Settlers arrived, Robert Hart was so intimately associated with them by marriage and otherwise, and proved a good a friend to many of them.

> *When the 1820 Settlers arrived in the Colony they found one man firmly established, with his roots sunk deep into the soil of the eastern frontier. Robert Hart, of Scotland, was to be remembered with gratitude by many a homesick 1820 Settler in the first tough years of hardship.*
>
> *With his diligence, scrupulous honesty, love of his fellow men and deep religious fervour, Hart, tempered by many years of stern army discipline, became a tremendous influence on the lives of all those around him.*[7]

Many years later, as 'Father of the Settlers', Robert Hart's bust, sculptured by Ivan Mitford Barberton, was placed in the vestibule of the 1820 Settler Memorial Hall in Grahamstown.

His first visit to the country was 25 years previous to this:

> *Private Robert Hart, just 18, and visibly Scottish from his rugged face to his green-and-black kilt, stared from the rolling deck at a phantom outline of peaks rising like clouds from the sea. To port and starboard, fore and*

---

7. *Father of the Settlers, Eastern Province Herald*, 13 June 1970. (Article by Pamela ffolliot)

aft, a fleet of many sail dipped and rose in the great green rollers. But it was the majestic coast, pallid with distance, standing up out of the sea to the eastward that held all eyes and arrested every mind on board the East Indiaman.

The end of four months' confinement, scurvy, and general misery in the troopship was in sight. What a breath-taking end that wild skyline of fantastic mountains looked, green and cold in the Cape spring of 1795![8]

---

8. *They Were South Africans*, John Bond, Oxford University Press, 1956

2.

Early Days

Robert Hart was born at Strathmore, Lanarkshire,[9] in 1777.[10] He was the elder of two sons from Presbyterian parents, Robert Hart, an ex-soldier reputed to have been a military man and a hard and ruthless parent and his wife, Mary Fleming.[11] The family moved to Edinburgh in 1783 and his mother died in 1791, when Robert was 14, and on her deathbed she begged him to remain at home. But because his home life was intolerable, and stirred by the martial enthusiasm of those times, Robert ran away the following year and enlisted. The first time he was sent home. His second attempt was more successful and he was enrolled as a private in the 91st regiment of the Argyll and Sutherland Highlanders, based at Stirling Castle, on 1 March 1794. This regiment had only just been formed – the 'muster roll' was opened on 8 February 1794 and Robert Hart was the 175th soldier to enlist on 1st March 1794. He was 17 years and 2 months old.

According to the War Office Register, a warrant for the raising of a Regiment of Foot under the command of Lt Col Duncan Campbell reads as follows:

Whereas we have though fit to raise a Regt of Foot to be forthwith raised

---

9. Lanarkshire, also called the County of Lanark, is a historic county in the central Lowlands of Scotland

10. His tombstone gives his date of birth as 1 Jan 1777 but according to an official document it was 5 January 1777

11. She was not Robert's mother but his step-mother who his father married after RH had already left

under your command, which is to consist of companies with 4 sergeants, 5 corporals, 2 drummers and 95 private men in each, with 2 Fifers to the Grenadier Company beside a Sergt Master and Quarter Master Sergt, together with the usual Commanding Officers. These are to authorise you by beat of drum or otherwise to raise so many men in any county or part of our Kingdom of Great Britain, as shall be wanted to complete the said Regt to the above-mentioned numbers.

Given at our Court of St James this 8th day of February 1794 in the 34th year of Our Reign.

By His Majesty's Command: Geo Younge.

After a period of training, the Regiment sailed to the Cape of Good Hope in an Indiaman[12] vessel, one of four transports under the command of General Clarke. On 4 September 1795 his troopship sailed into False Bay with 13 others to relieve the tiny British force which had captured Muizenberg. The plight of General Craig's little force, clinging to its toehold on Simon's Bay, had reached General Clarke on the voyage south. By now it might have been wiped out by lack of supplies and by superior numbers.

Indiaman vessel

---

12. (East) Indiaman was a general name for any sailing ship operating under charter or licence to any of the East India Companies of the major European trading powers of the 17th to the 19th centuries. These include the Danish, Dutch, English, French, Portuguese and Swedish East India companies

A glance at the current state of affairs in Europe is necessary here. In the winter of 1794, during the French Revolutionary Wars, French troops entered the Dutch Republic, following which the Prince of Orange fled to England. Given the turmoil in Europe and the importance of the Cape sea-route to India the British Government launched operations against the Dutch Empire to gain use of its facilities against the French Navy. Sir Francis Baring, chairman of the English East India Company, put it succinctly in a January 1795 letter to the British Secretary of State for War, Henry Dundas, when he pointed out that the Cape, commands the passage to and from India as effectively as Gibraltar does the Mediterranean. Equally trenchantly, Dundas's Under-Secretary noted that although the Cape was 'a feather in the hands of the Dutch' it would become 'a sword in the hands of France'.[13]

At the Cape, the person in charge of the VOC's affairs was Commissioner-General Abraham Sluysken. Sluysken had taken over the government of the Cape Colony under circumstances of great difficulty.[14] *The credit of the East India Company was exhausted, and its debt was ten million pounds sterling. In February 1794 it was obliged to declare itself unable to meet the interest on its loans. To maintain a garrison capable of defending the country in case of attack was beyond its power.*

He was not aware of the events in Europe and was still under the impression that the British were allies and the French were enemies of the Dutch.

Admiral Sir George Keith Elphinstone[15] sailed up to the anchorage in Simon's Bay on 9 June 1795 in command of nine vessels, having on board troops under the command of Major-General James Henry Craig. Elphinstone's fleet reached the Cape in a poor state: in need of

---

13. South African Military History Society, *Military History Journal*, Vol 13 No 4 - Dec 2005

14. From the official records of the Dutch East India Company's administration as recorded by George McCall Theal (1837-1919). Theal was Keeper of the Cape Colony Archives and in 1891 he was appointed Colonial Historiographer

15. South African Military History Society Newsletter No 452 - April 2017

provisions and water but without funds to buy necessities, and hundreds of sailors and soldiers sick with scurvy. What is more, Craig's force lacked field guns and land transport. On 11 June the arrival of warships under 'unrecognisable flags' was reported from Simon's Bay, the VOC's winter harbour.

Elphinstone

Elphinstone invited Sluysken to visit the flagship to discuss with him the Prince's instruction to receive the British fleet and troops as those of an allied power sent to prevent the Cape form falling into French hands. He presented the Governor a letter[16] emphasizing the advantages of British protection to the House of Orange, signed by Prince Willem. This missive invited the Government and inhabitants of the settlement of the Cape of Good Hope 'to accept and put themselves under the protection of His said Majesty by delivering up the said settlement with its dependencies to the forces under our respective command in order to prevent its falling into the hands of the Enemy and to be held for the purpose aforesaid until a general pacification shall have composed the differences now subsisting in Europe.

---

16. Sir George Cory, Volume 6 of *The Rise of South Africa: A History of the Origin of South African Colonisation and of Its Development Towards the East from the Earliest Times to 1857*, Struik, 1965

What Elphinstone concealed was that the government in the Netherlands had not only changed hands but also allies. This was only revealed at the end of June, when a Dutch newspaper got through the British blockade. The stadtholder system had been abolished, Dutch subjects at home and abroad were absolved of their allegiance to the House of Orange and most of the population in the Netherlands had welcomed the French as liberators.

Mr Sluysken, while expressing his gratitude for such kind consideration, intimated that the military strength of the Colony was sufficient for its own protection, and that in the event of difficulty arising he would gladly avail himself of the proffered assistance. However, he soon became suspicious of the real motives of the English and, quickly terminating the supplies to Elphinstone's ships, adopted an aggressive stance. Burghers were summoned from the far-lying districts by means of fires lit on the hill-tops to support the military in resisting the looming invasion. But the response was lukewarm to say the least; there was too much dissatisfaction with the Dutch authorities.

The battle that was to follow had a profound effect on the history of the colony. As John Bond[17] wrote:

> *It was much more than a battle that Robert Hart and his 800 comrades were sailing into across the heaving floor of False Bay. It was a thunderclap that would end the immemorial sleep of the Dark Continent. The Dutch East India Company was weighed in the balance that day and found wanting. The outpost of Christian civilisation which it had founded in Africa, and which it had failed, was passing for good or evil to stronger hands. Robert Moffat and the Great Trek; Livingstone breaking through from the Voortrekkers' farthest north to the Great Lakes and the Congo; Rhodes drawing the steel threads of his railway into the Kingdom of Monomotapa, and his telegraph line to the fountains of the Nile: all this*

---

17. *They Were South Africans*, John Bond, Oxford University Press, 1956

and more was decided on that day that Robert Hart would never forget, the fourth of September 1795.

Six days of wild rumours elapsed, with the fleet rocking at anchor in Simon's Bay, before Robert Hart's regiment carried their kit ashore. Five days followed of desperately heavy work man-handling guns, ammunition, and stores along the beaches to Muizenberg. Men's labour, General Clarke noted grimly, was 'the only means in our power' of transporting the whole impedimenta of the army along the rock-bound coast which has since become the Riviera of Africa.

At dawn on 14 September the Argyllshire Highlanders set out from Muizenburg to occupy Cape Town in the name of King George and on behalf of His Serene Highness the Prince of Orange.

For lack of horses, seamen hauled the guns. The troops themselves staggered under their loads across the marshy flats in full view and range of Commissioner-General Sluysken's Hottentot sharp-shooters, mounted farmers, and mutinous German mercenaries. Bullets whistled over the heads of the 98th. But there was no fight in the defenders, for the colony of the Cape of Good Hope was even more rent with dissensions than was French-occupied Holland. After a final skirmish at Wynberg the mercenaries turned and ran, and Sluysken sent in his flag of truce. The same Providence which, 143 years before, had permitted van Riebeeck to plant a Dutch settlement in the remotest tip of Africa now permitted a second European race to make its home in South Africa.

The 98th occupied the Castle which was to be their base for the next seven years.

3.

Colonel Gordon
and the Battle of Muizenburg

Colonel Robert Jacob Gordon, although of Scottish descent, was a Dutch explorer, soldier, artist, naturalist and linguist. His father commanded the Scots Brigade in the service of the Netherlands.

He had already visited the Cape several times previously and was acknowledged as the foremost authority with respect to the interior of southern Africa of his time. He was the first person to record finding fossils in South Africa[18] and once devoted the best part of a day to examining a hippo's entrails, and sent back to Holland the hide of the last giraffe shot south of the Orange.[19] He made meticulous observations

18. Ron Maclennan, *The Wind Makes Dust*, Tafelberg, 2003

19. However, according to *Historical Incidence of the Larger Land Mammals in the broader Eastern Cape*, CJ Skead, 'no proof that this animal ever occurred south of the Orange River.'

of the geography, fauna, flora, weather and native inhabitants of the regions he visited. In 1779 he renamed the Kai !Garib (Kariep) River of the Orange, after the Dutch Royal House, and followed it to its mouth.

But later, as a military officer, he was sent back by the directors of the Dutch East India Company, soon to command the Cape garrison. Here he was in some conflict with the Governor who was ultimately responsible for the defence of the colony. He clashed with Governors Van Plettenberg and Van de Graaff but seemed to be given more respect by the recently-arrived Governor Slusyken. He accompanied him to the meeting with Elphinstone.

Once the Prince's letter had been rejected, Gordon took command of the field forces[20] to resist the invasion.

Elphinstone was not in favour of a sea-borne attack on Cape Town itself because Table Bay was unsafe in winter, and its shores were in any case protected by a line of heavy defence works, including the Castle and the Sea Line, a stone wall with gun batteries to prevent landings. His only remaining option was an overland attack that involved soldiers, weighed down by their equipment, hauling field guns the forty kilometres over the rough terrain from Simon's Bay to Cape Town.

Dan Sleigh[21] writes:

> *In a first aggressive act the British in Simon's Bay seized VOC ships (two outward-bound, three homeward) and put prize crews on them. Next, they became masters of the port without any effort on their part when Sluysken withdrew his troops from Simon's Bay to Muysenburg, without a shot being fired. On 14 July British troops landed to occupy the VOC's abandoned facilities. They now fed from the Company's stores*

---

20. His military strength comprised 1 741 infantry, 900 cavalry and 990 gunners with field pieces and cannons of various calibres

21. Much of this chapter is attributed to Dr Dan Sleigh, the internationally-acknowledged historian and the foremost authority on the history of the Dutch East Indies Company during the 17th and 18th centuries at the Cape. Daniel holds a BA Degree in History and English Literature (UNISA) and a Doctorate in History (University of Stellenbosch)

and vegetable gardens, carpenters built gun carriages and handcarts in the workshops for a march on Cape Town and boats crews took soundings off Muysenburg beach to see how close ships could approach for a bombardment of the Dutch camp.

Battle of Muizenberg

The attack on Muysenburg began on 7 August. With Elphinstone in charge, four warships fired at the camp while sixteen hundred British soldiers advanced by road, unopposed. Lieutenant-Colonel De Lille, the VOC officer who substituted for Gordon, led his confused troops in flight, leaving field guns, provision wagons and tents standing. 'The Dutch on our approach neither behaved with courage or prudence, nor took proper advantage of their strong positions.' wrote a British eyewitness.

Three thousand British reinforcements arrived in early September, and their commander, General Clarke, notified Sluysken that he had orders to attack at once if he found the Cape still in Dutch hands. Sluysken reiterated his resolve to defend the Cape but did not order Gordon to employ and lead his troops; instead he wasted his forces in idleness, exposing them to the winter rain, until every single advantage was lost. In spite of strong burgher protests, Sluysken persisted to the end with absent and inept officers.

However, Sluysken eventually had to capitulate on 16 September when the burgher forces abandoned the campaign and went home, unwilling to become prisoners of war. 'The next day Colonel Gordon came forward to lead the troops for the first time, to lay down their arms and be taken prisoners of war. And that was the only time he drew his sword. He died by his own hand, shortly after the British takeover.'

Although Gordon had sworn allegiance to the Lords Seventeen, the States-General and Prince Willem V, while a cadet in the Scots Brigade, he had also sworn allegiance to the King of England, as was expected of its officers. Elphinstone and Craig had 'grounds for hoping' that he would join them with his troops when they landed and, when military action commenced, believed that they could count on Gordon's Anglophile sympathies to defect. Colonel Gordon had already written privately to Elphinstone: 'I shall serve the Common cause with all my exertions [but] prudence is necessary to bring things to a proper end,' and: 'I abhor French principles and if our unhappy republic... should surrender...then I am a Great Britainer.'

Gordon could have resigned on the strength of the oath to do so when personal scruples clashed with loyalty. He did not resign, but neither did he fight. While his troops were in action Gordon avoided the front and

Prince of Orange

also absented himself from strategic discussions. He had a last chance to stand by his vaunted loyalty to the Prince of Orange by rejecting the capitulation that made no mention of Prince Willem or the eventual return of the Cape to the Dutch government. Instead, he signed it.

After the surrender, Gordon was socially disgraced, reviled by the garrison and became spiritually depressed. He was attacked and beaten in the street. Former subordinates such as Engineer Captain LM Thibault, Artillery Lieutenant P Marnitz and Sergeant HD Campagne wrote disparagingly of his conduct. Their testimonies coincided, and they did not hide their frustration, indignation and contempt; to them the Colonel's behaviour during the invasion was inexplicable, irregular and unsoldierly. Sir John Malcolm, who was attached to General Clarke's staff, and so involved in the advance on Cape Town, wrote that Gordon neglected his duty. Imagine that this officer was President of a court martial, with Gordon on the carpet. What would the verdict be? Dr Sleigh pointed out that three senior British officers had been executed for cowardice: Captains Richard Kirby and Cooper Wade in 1701, and Admiral John Byng in 1757.

Colonel Gordon committed suicide on 25 October 1795.

Early photo of Graaff-Reinet

4.

Conflict in Graaff-Reinet

What were Hart's first impressions of Cape Town in 1795?

The crowds of slaves, brown, black, and yellow, and the ragged, yellow-faced Hottentots cheering and laughing along the road? The white burghers' families, silently watching in their eighteenth-century finery? Or the great gallows close to the Castle, with crows settled on the corpses swinging there, and the blood-stained wheels below on which slaves were broken for raising a hand to their masters?

The neat lines of shapely whitewashed houses with green shutters made a pleasant picture under Table Mountain. Vines were covering trellises with new leaf. The scent of orange blossom, strange to Scottish nostrils, drifted alluringly down straight roads lined with oaks in young green.

'Here is a divine climate, no fog, no damp . . . but a clean, pure yet not sharp air, full of health and exhilaration to the spirits,' wrote Lady Anne Barnard, whom Hart often saw from a respectful distance after her arrival as first lady of the Colony. 'The town is clean . . . the features upon Nature's face magnificently strong.'[22]

The 98th was on standby for further invasion and, less than a year from their arrival, heard the news that the Batavian Republic had sent out Admiral de Winter to retake the Cape Colony and had put into Saldanha Bay. Coincidentally a fleet from England with troops going to India had just put into Simons Bay for supplies. These troops were landed, and 2 000, along with the 98th, started foot-slogging their way across the heavy sands of the Cape Flats – there was still no road – en route to

---

22. *They Were South Africans*, John Bond

Saldanha Bay overland, and Admiral de Winter's fleet slipped its moorings and sailed up the coast to shut up the Dutch fleet in the Bay. The column arrived nine days later to witness the surrender of the trapped Dutch fleet, six sail-of-the-line and two frigates. In 1798 turbulence in the district of Graaff-Reinet required military intervention. The disturbances had started back in 1795, when the burghers expelled the Landdrost Maynier and proclaimed an independent 'Colony of Graaff-Reinet,' requesting guardianship under the government in the Netherlands (and not the VOC). Similar action was subsequently taken by the burghers of Swellendam. Before the authorities at Cape Town could take decisive measures against the rebels they were themselves compelled to capitulate to the British who invaded and occupied the Cape.

Now the British Government reacted with the despatch of a store-ship of 14 guns from Table Bay to Algoa Bay with a detachment of troops, consisting of two flank companies of the 98th Regiment, a few artillerymen with two nine-pounders and, overland, a squadron of the 8th Dragoons and a body of the Cape Regiment, under the command of Brigadier General Van de Leur.[23]

The detachment was sent by sea to a landing-place at the mouth of the Baakens River in Algoa Bay where Port Elizabeth now stands. On arrival they proceeded across country from the Bay which took them through wild country, abounding in animals of all sorts, including lions and great herds of elephant. Wandering Bushmen and hostile natives were also an ever present hazard. Hart, with his love of flora and fauna, was keenly aware both of the profusion of flowers that carpeted much of the ground, and of the strangely different bushes and trees that covered the countryside.[24]

The following is an account of the situation as related by Robert Hart,

---

23. General Sir John Ormsby Van de Leur (1763 – 1849), was a British Army officer who fought in the French Revolutionary and Napoleonic wars

24. Talk by Mrs. Doris Craib at the Somerset East Museum's Annual General Meeting in March 1977

shortly before his death at the age of 90, to John Centlivers Chase.[25]

> *The Grenadiers and Light Infantry of the 98th landed at Algoa Bay
> and took up their quarters about five miles from the port at some fine
> springs of water, where they found one Thomas Ferreira in possession. The
> troops from their overland route united at this place, and before proceeding
> on their further expedition they here entrenched themselves by surrounding
> Ferreira's hut with earthworks the remains of which (Star Fort) are still
> visible, cut deep into the soil at Cradock Place, thus establishing this spot
> as the first military headquarters in the Eastern part of the Colony. From
> this, early in 1799, they proceeded towards Graaff-Reinet, endeavouring
> en route to surprising some of the ringleaders, who had taken up position
> between that town and the sea, but without effect. Van de Leur then issued
> a Proclamation, requiring submission and inviting farmers in revolt to meet
> him at the farm of William Prinsloo on Bruintjies Hoogte (which adjoined
> the farm that Hart was later to acquire) as the most central spot. Sixteen
> of the insurgents had in the interim fled into Kafirland but, after some little
> hesitation, on the day appointed (6th April) the greater number assembled
> and lay down their arms; a few were taken into custody and sent to Cape
> Town, where they remained prisoners in the Castle until the Colony was
> given up to the Batavian Government in 1803.*

Bond: *Destiny led the company from Graaff-Reinet itself, where rebellion
> dispersed at the sight of the redcoats, eastwards past Bruintjies Hoogte in
> pursuit of Prinsloo and van Jaarsveld, to a beautiful mountain. Clothed
> in forest and flecked with waterfalls, the Boschberg towered above the valley
> it watered, looking, after the scorching Karroo, like a vision of Eden. There
> Prinsloo and van Jaarsveld were satisfactorily arrested. And there, eighteen
> years later, Hart and his wife Hannah with their bevy of children would
> make their home—the home that grew into Somerset East.*
>
> *From the Boschberg, Hart's company marched at leisure southwards*

---

25. Old Times and Odd Corners, John Centlivres Chase, Historical Society of Port Elizabeth & Walmer 1969

and westwards towards Algoa Bay with the rest of General Van de Leur's force. They passed tall forests and hills covered with grass and flowers. This green Zuurveld, still the home of the elephant, would become in another twenty years the cradle-land of the English-speaking South African. Its green grass, its little mountain streams and primeval forests, were an invitation then as now to the English South African spirit. Wherever you find that combination in South Africa you will also hear the English tongue.

The men of the 98th—but by now it had been renumbered the 91st— were seeing at last the good lands of Africa that lie beyond the moat of deserts which protected the infant settlement of the Cape. Here, where the green grass begins, they clashed almost at once with the outposts of the advancing Bantu race, whose dominions stretched southward from the Mountains of the Moon.

Sundays River

At the Sundays River, Hart's company with the rest of Van de Leur's column were attacked by tribesmen hurling assegais and shouting. The troops retaliated with gunfire and the attackers fled. Lieutenant Chumney and his detachment of the 81st had pitched camp on the Bushman's

River when hundreds of Cungwa's[26] warriors streamed out of the bush with their short assegais and cattle-hide shields to assail the British. They were repulsed with volleys of musket-balls and grape-shot. This heralded what was known as the Third Kaffir War.

Warriors

'At every farmer's house', one of Hart's comrades recorded in his description of that disastrous war, 'we found sad vestiges of murder and desolation. Whole families had been wantonly massacred . . . A poor dog might be found howling over the dead body of his master or some wounded horse or ox groaning with the stab of a spear. The savage Cafir exults in such appalling sights.'

The old veteran - but at that time a young man of 23 - Mr Hart then adds another episode to his personal recollections of this period while he was at this Fort at Papenkuil's Fontein, nothing less than a veritable sea-fight in Algoa Bay, where lay the Rattlesnake frigate and the Camel, quite unconscious of approaching danger.

What happened was that a French frigate entered the Bay from the east under British colours. She dropped anchor alongside the Camel. After dark she ran up the Tricolor and fired a broadside into that ship. The Rattlesnake could do little as her crew was on shore. Two nine-pounders

---

26. Cungwa was head of the Gunukwebe (amaGqunukhwebe) clan, next to Ndlambe the most powerful chief west of the Fish River

> *were loaded on a wagon and brought down to the shore and fired. The French ship withdrew and it was subsequently ascertained she was La Preneuse of 48 guns heavy metal.*[27]

Algoa Bay had already been recognised as an ideal landing-place and port for the East and General Van der Leur decided to erect a permanent military post there. A wooden blockhouse, capable of holding sixty men, had been constructed at considerable cost in Cape Town and sent round in pieces on board the Camel. It was put together on the low ground near the ford across the Baaken's River, close to the sea-shore. It was armed with two three-pounders and thus formed a protection to the chief supply of fresh water.

In the gruelling months that followed, Hart spent many months in the mobile force which General Dundas mustered, along with Boer commandos and the Hottentot Corps in fruitless attacks on the Xhosa forces of Ndlambi.[28] Hart was exposed to constant danger to which the frontier farmers of South Africa had been subjected. Battle-hardened, it was no wonder that, 20 years on, he was described by Thomas Pringle as, 'a man of iron look and rigid nerve'.

A despatch came from England early in the year 1803 ordering the Colony to be given over to the Dutch. After some seven years in South Africa the Argyllshires were ordered to sail for India where trouble had broken out. At the end of a spell of two years the men were sent back to England, via the Cape.

The story is told of how, soon after Hart's arrival, he was best man at a friend's wedding. Turning to another friend he remarked, 'The man's a fool, I'd rather have the bridesmaid.' Robert must have been a fast worker because he married the bridesmaid, a certain Hannah May

---

27. *Old Times & Odd Corners*

28. Ndhlambi was a man of considerable ability and withal a bold warrior; albeit at times his valour got the better of his discretion and brought about disaster. He became the most powerful chief in Kaffirland and the one who gave the greatest trouble, both directly and indirectly, to the British Government in subsequent years. (*The Rise of South Africa*, GB Cory)

Tamplin, at Port St. Peters, Guernsey, on 10 April 1804. The young lady, from Charlwood, Surrey, was to be the perfect wife and helpmate until her death 49 years later. The newly-wed couple enjoyed some two years of peaceful army life in England, until, receiving his commission, Sergeant-Major Hart was sent back to South Africa, to join Colonel John Graham[29] in the recently formed Cape Regiment. (Hart had served with the 1st British Battalion in Hanover, Germany, returning to England in February 1806 and so joined the second occupation of the Cape late, in 1807).

Colonel Graham, travelling from Cape Town to the eastern districts with a corps of Khoikhoi troops, came to the Palmiet River which had no bridge. The owner of the ferry was reluctant to allow people of colour to use his boat. Graham confessed to his diary that he could not avoid a feeling of 'inward satisfaction at the spirit his men showed there'.[30]

> *The owner of the boat made a bitter complaint against some of our Hottentot soldiers who were going on pass who he said had not only been extremely unruly and troublesome in his house by insisting on having wine (which he allowed they had paid for) but what seemed to offend his feelings still more they carried his boat to the opposite side of the river where having arrived in safety they were ill-mannered enough to draw up in line on top of the bank and expose their Bare Breach for the inspection of the half-caste gentleman above alluded to.*

---

29. Colonel John Graham, thirteenth Laird of Fintry, was one of the most distinguished soldiers who ever fought on the frontier. He had commanded a battalion of the Light Infantry Brigade with distinction at the Battle of Blaauwberg Strand in 1806

30. Ben Maclennan, *The Wind Makes Dust*

SADF Cape Corps emblem

5.

Adjutant of the Cape Corps

General Baird

In 1806 General Baird retook the Cape for the British Government, but Hart was not present on that occasion, for after remaining a little while in England he went with the Highlanders to Hanover where he stayed for a short time when Napoleon vacated the country.

Hart shared cantonment life with his wife for a tranquil year and a half in England while a new war with Napoleon raged on the Continent. All through the summer of 1806 the 91st were in strict training at Shorncliffe camp, under the great Sir John Moore himself. It was in July at Shorncliffe that a summons arrived from Cape Town which Robert and Hannah had doubtless long been expecting. Sergeant-Major Hart, it announced, had been given his commission in Colonel John Graham's newly founded Cape Regiment. An incident on the voyage to the Cape reflects the softer side of Robert Hart.[31]

After his regiment went on to India Graham was ordered to remain behind for special duty: the governor was looking for someone to re-organise the Cape Corps, which had fallen on evil days. His choice fell on Graham, and the latter soon justified the high opinion which had been formed of him. Under his command the raw Hottentot levies were turned into first-class soldiers and the regiment as a whole into an efficient fighting force. This then was the man appointed by Sir John Cradock to perform the stupendous task of restoring the white man's supremacy in the East.

To carry out the invasion of the Zuurveld, Graham split his troops into three divisions. The right wing was under Major JG Cuyler, the Landdrost of Uitenhage, the centre under himself and Captain GS Fraser, and the left wing under Landdrost Andries Stockenström of Graaff-Reinet, who was destined to lose his life under the most tragic circumstances during the course of the campaign.

The events leading up to the involvement of coloured people in the military dates back to about 1796 when the Government of the Colony employed a few Hottentots to carry messages and in the following year the British troops being encamped in the middle of the village of Stellenbosch under Lieut Colonel King, Hottentots came from their Chiefs from various parts and mingled with the soldiers in order to get food and countenance, as they were at that time very badly used by the Dutch.[32]

Then Hottentots at last became so numerous to be troublesome and Colonel King ordered an officer of the Highlanders to collect them and inform them that they might carry messages and collect information.

---

31. On a previous voyage to the Cape the plague broke out on the ship and carried off many of the passengers. Amongst others a family named McInnes perished, with the exception of a little boy and his younger sister. The kindly nature of the young lieutenant was shown by his taking upon himself the responsibility of his countryman's forlorn little orphans. He brought them to the Cape, had them educated while here, and eventually sent them to their relatives in Scotland

32. Sir Gordon Sprigg

On these circumstances being represented to the Home Government it was proposed to form them into a corps being formed upward of 100 strong, and this was the origin of the regiment now known by the name of the Cape Mounted Riflemen. After that an order came from the Horse Guards to form a regiment of 10 companies. This was hardly done before the Treaty of Amiens was concluded and the Colony given over to the Dutch.

But the regiment continued to exist and on the occasion of the recapture of the Colony by General Baird, the Cape Corps came over bodily to the English. They were, however, at that time merely an assembly of people, being only partially trained. In the year 1807 on his return to the Colony, Mr Hart was selected for a commission in the Cape Corps and was appointed Adjutant to the regiment, and with this regiment he remained until they were disbanded in 1817.

For considerably over a century the coloured manhood of South Africa has rendered military service in the defence of the country.[33]

Ivor Difford writes:

From 1795 to the present day, in the innumerable native wars and disturbances, coloured men have borne their share. In the more recent campaigns, subsequent to 1854, their service, whilst not combatant, has been of great value and in the transport organisation they have proved a valuable auxiliary, but it was not until the great world war, now happily at an end, that they had the opportunity of showing their value as fighting material on a similar footing to their European brethren in arms, and the services they have rendered in that great conflict have been of the greatest value and won the highest encomiums of their commanding generals and officers.

---

33. *The Story of the 1st Battalion Cape Corps (1815-1819)* by Captain Ivor D. Difford, Quartermaster, 1st Cape Corps, 1915-1919. Cape Town, Hortors, 1920

Ivor Difford's book

Difford placed on record their contribution to the defence of South Africa from the earliest period, very few years having passed without a coloured corps being engaged in one or other of the warlike operations against the natives which were such a feature in the history of the Cape in the early and mid-nineteenth century.

The first official cognisance of the use of coloured men, either Hottentots or mixed descent, in a military capacity would appear to have been in 1795 when Commissioner Sluyskens embodied a corps of *Pandours*[34] and used them in his operations against the British, including at Kalk Bay on 7 August 1795. At this period the uniform consisted of a short scarlet jacket with yellow collars and cuffs and trimmed with a kind of white lace, blue cloth trousers with a black and red stripe and a round felt hat.

When the British took over at the Cape Coloured levies were induced to enter the British service, and in April, 1796, coloured men presented themselves at the quarters of the Light Infantry Brigade under Major King at Stellenbosch. At first these men were employed as cooks, but

---

34. The term was originally used for soldiers in Hungary, from a Serbo-Croatian word for a mounted policeman

their number increased and they were embodied into a corps under Lieutenant John Campbell of the 98th Foot with a sergeant of the same regiment. Additional officers and NCOs were attached and the corps was stationed at Hout Bay. The men were enlisted for one year and provided with arms, clothing and rations and the munificent sum of sixpence a week in money. Their service was for the interior of the Colony, and the primary object of their enlistment would appear to have been in connection with the refusal of the burghers at Graaff-Reinet to take the oath of allegiance to King-George III.

They are next referred to in March 1799, when a detachment was sent to Graaff-Reinet to suppress the rebellion there. They were under the command of Brigadier-General Van de Leur, who took a strong detachment of dragoons and a party of the coloured *Pandours* overland from Cape Town. Parties also left on board the *Star* and the *Hope* and landed at Algoa Bay. In 1799 the Cape Corps, under General Van de Leur, took part in the operations against the Kaffir chiefs Ndlambe and the rebellious Hottentots. In 1800 the men were formed into a regiment under the command of Lieut Colonel King, with Major D. Campbell as second in command. Their headquarters were at Groenekloof, near Cape Town, detachments being stationed at Graaff-Reinet and Port Elizabeth.

Värmland

Mounted commandos

Bruintjies Hoogte

6.

Anders and Andries Stockenström

On the website, *Armoria Familia, The Baronets Stockenström*, Mike Oettle writes:

> *Born at Filipstad in Värmland, Sweden, on 6 January 1757, Anders was the son of Anders Andersen Stockenström (1707-1764), inspector of mines and mayor of Filipstad, and Caterina Margarita Ekman. In September 1781 Anders sailed from Texel (an island off the Netherlands coast) as a quarter-gunner aboard a VOC ship, 't Zeepaard.*

Anders, after serving with the military forces of the VOC, later worked in the goods office in Cape Town and was bookkeeper to the company fleet. In 1786 he married Maria Geertruyda Broeders, daughter of Peter Caspar Brodersen from Rantrum, a North Frisian town in Schleswig, and Elsabe Cornelia Colijn. The couple had four sons and four daughters.

After the British occupation of the Cape in 1795 General Craig appointed him secretary to Landdrost AA Faure, of Swellendam. Following the takeover of the Cape by the Batavian Republic, Anders was retained by the new administration and appointed Landdrost of Graaff-Reinet by Governor Jan Willem Janssens and Commissioner-General Jacob Abraham Uitenhage de Mist swore him in on 14 February 1804, at which time Graaff-Reinet had been without a permanent landdrost since 1801.Two years later he was an assistant in the *negotie comptoir* (goods office) in Cape Town, where he remained for some years. He also served as supercargo on a vessel carrying slaves for the VOC from Madagascar to the Cape, and was afterwards, until 1795 (when the British captured the Cape), bookkeeper to the fleet.

His eight years as landdrost – under Batavian rule until 1806, and then under British rule – saw the district experiencing Bushman raids in the north and north-west, and an unsettled frontier with the amaXhosa. While commandos were sent against the Bushmen, Anders also tried to reconcile the Bushmen by having game shot for them, and periodically giving them cattle.

When action was eventually taken against the Xhosa in December 1811, Anders, in command of the burghers of Graaff-Reinet, occupied Bruintjies Hoogte to protect the area north of the Zuurberg. The commandos of George, Uitenhage and Swellendam, together with the Cape Regiment, gathered at the Sundays River mouth and after Christmas, crossed the river to expel the Xhosa from the Addo bush

On 27 December Col John Graham of Fintry sent orders to Stockenström to join the rest of the force at Coerney, where Col J G Cuyler (landdrost of Uitenhage) was in charge. Realising that this would leave the area north of the Zuurberg vulnerable to Xhosa attack, Anders went to discuss the matter with Graham.

When steps were eventually taken against the Xhosa in December 1811, Anders, in command of the burghers of Graaff-Reinet, occupied Bruintjies Hoogte to protect the area north of the Zuurberg. The commandos of George, Uitenhage and Swellendam, together with the Cape Regiment, gathered at the Sundays River mouth and after Christmas, crossed the river to drive the Xhosa from the Addo bush.

Stockenström, realising that this would leave the area north of the Zuurberg vulnerable to Xhosa attack, set out on 29 December 1811 with 24 men. About five hours later he encountered a number of Xhosa on

Doringnek, the watershed between the White and Coerney rivers, on the Zuurberg. Relying on his popularity as the friend and benefactor of both colonists and indigenous peoples, Anders dismounted and went to meet the war party unarmed. He spent at least half an hour endeavouring to persuade Chief Kasa to return to their country without bloodshed. But when he returned to mount his horse, the Imidange had surrounded his party and attacked, killing him, eight burghers and an interpreter. Four were wounded but managed to escape.

In the younger Stockenström's autobiography[35], he referred to the little-known rumour that the Dutch authorities had actually sold the Zuurveld to the Xhosas. He wrote:

The causes and necessity of the war were amply discussed. Some of the elders of the Boers maintained that we were not altogether in the right. A few even protested that they firmly believed that the Kaffirs did buy the Zuurveld from the Dutch authorities, and two or three of them affirmed with oaths that they had seen in certain herds some of the oxen which had been received in payment; some as firmly denied this altogether, and I may here observe that I had previously, and have subsequently heard the allegation as well as the denial a hundred times. My father had no faith in it, but said: 'if even the slightest doubt exist, so much the more is it our duty as Christians and civilised men to try and get this question settled without bloodshed, and if I can manage to get a sight of Habana and Kasa and the other Chiefs on my way tomorrow, I shall certainly do my best to induce them to evacuate the disputed territory under a solemn promise that the strictest enquiry shall be instituted, and that if they can prove the purchase and payment full compensation shall be made. Eight hundred oxen are worth some twenty thousand rix dollars, and what is this to the mighty British Government in the cause of humanity and justice. 'He went into his tent and slept for the last time till peep of day, the 28th December, 1811.'

---

35. Hutton, C. W. The Hon. (Editor) *The Autobiography Of The Late Sir Andries Stockenström, Bart,* 2 Vols

In 1821 Thomas Pringle, accompanied by Robert Hart, visited the spot where Anders Stockenström lost his life ten years previously. The following graphic account is taken from Pringle's subsequent description of the tragedy:[36]

Thomas Pringle

Leaving his camp in charge of his son, Ensign Andries Stockenström, he set out at daybreak on 29 December 1811 with an escort of forty men. Their journey lay among some of the wildest, most rugged and yet most magnificent scenery in the whole of Southern Africa. For five hours they toiled through gigantic kloofs, covered with dense, almost impenetrable undergrowth or skirted huge forests of lofty yellowwood trees, while overhead towered the massive crags and pinnacles of the Zuurberg Range, until at last they reached a narrow ridge, suspended high above two mighty arms of the mountain chain which it connected.

When Stockenström's party neared this dangerous pass, they saw that large bodies of armed Kafirs had collected on either side of the narrow

36. Pringle's *Narrative of a Residence in South Africa*

ridge which they would have to traverse. In the midst of this mountain scenery we arrived at a spot where the elder Stockenström, landdrost of Graaff-Reinet, had been slain by the Caffers in 1811. Mr Hart, who had served in the colonial campaign of that period under Colonel Graham, related to me the circumstances of this melancholy affair as we rode along. The tragic scene was brief. Mr Stockenström and fourteen of his men fell, pierced by innumerable wounds.

When Anders Stockenström was murdered, Andries was his father's aide-de-camp. When the news of the incident reached Bruintjies Hoogte, Andries and 18 mounted burghers rode in haste to Doringnek. There they surprised a number of the killers, killed 13 and recovered eight horses. Following the Doringnek incident Andries was appointed to his father's position in command of the burgher forces.

Stockenström

AH Duminy writes:[37]

In May 1815 Lord Charles Somerset, on the recommendation of his predecessors the Earl of Caledon and Sir John Cradock, appointed him. landdrost of the district of Graaff-Reinet. Thus, at the age of twenty-two, he became the chief instrument of British policy in this vast frontier district whose inhabitants had scarcely experienced effective government, and which bordered on the Bushmen and Griquas to the and on the Bantu to the east. It was his responsibility not only to regulate relations between the colonists and the border tribes, but to implement the policies of the British authorities. These included, in particular, the substitution of perpetual quit-rent land tenure for the existing loan-place system; the provision of educational facilities; and the extension of the protection law to the Hottentots and other coloured inhabitants. The difficulties involved were demonstrated by the Slagtersnek rebellion, which occurred in November 1815 (shortly after Stockenström's appointment) when he helped significantly to dissuade the colonists from joining the projected rebellion and to bring the rebels to peace.

In 1817 the 'commando system', which had operated on the frontier and which depended on the civil authority of the landdrost, who could authorize armed expeditions across the frontier to retake stolen stock, was replaced with the 'reprisals system'. In terms of this new system, of which Stockenström remained an outspoken critic, burgher patrols were to be accompanied by a military detachment and were entitled to demand compensation from the kraal to which the spoor of stolen cattle had been traced, whether or not the stolen stock was found there, leaving the Xhosa to find the guilty and claim their cattle back from them.

(See Appendix)

---

37. Duminy was a contributor to the *Dictionary of South African Biography*, editor, W J De Kock; National Council for Social Research (South Africa), published by Nasional Boekhandel Bpk for National Council for Social Research, Dept. of Higher Education [1968-1987]

Sir Charles Somerset

When Sir Charles Somerset heard that some thousands of British settlers were to be on his hands to be located in the Colony. He summoned Stockenström as he assumed that land must be plentiful in the Graaff-Reinet district, for up to that period not many quit-rent titles had been issued. However the latter stated there was no land for British settlers in this district.

As Stockenström recorded in his autobiography:

The Governor, drawing up with prodigious dignity, said, 'But you must know, sir, that the landdrosts are strictly forbidden to allow the occupation of Government land.' I then for the first time in my life felt myself stung by higher authority, and, likewise drawing up with due humility, said: 'I do know it, my lord — forbidden on pain of dismissal from office; but the Colonial Secretary might have told your Lordship that that occupation took place long before I had anything to do with the district; that the Government knew it; that it was notorious; that Sir J. Cradock's proclamation gave those occupants reasonable hope that where the application was not immoderate it would be granted, provided the applicant should comply with the quit-rent regulations; that numerous petitions were at once sent in on the faith of that proclamation; that in many instances the pecuniary deposits have already been made; in some cases the lands have been already surveyed, and in most cases the people are prepared to do everything the said law prescribes, and I can only assure your lordship that if the squatters be driven from those lands, they have no alternative except migrating beyond the frontier, and coming into collision with the native tribes, and that at any rate for me it will be impossible to make the old established Boer give way to the newcomers.'

The Secretary said nothing. The Governor, meeting with no support from that quarter, became calm, and said: 'What is to be done with these settlers? Here is Colonel Bird maintaining that I have no right to locate them in the territory between the Fish River and the Keiskamma.'

I have so fully stated to the Committee of the Commons what took place on this subject, that I shall not repeat it here; but when His Excellency spoke about the Zuurveld I gave it as my opinion that it would be dangerous to place the settlers in close contact with the Kaffirs, as they would be no match for the barbarians in case of inroads. I suggested that as they were likely to be a great part sea-faring men, or people from near sea-ports, they would like to possess Mossel Bay, Plettenberg Bay, the Knysna, and Algoa Bay, and that plenty of land would be found for them in and between those parts, as a great part of the land was still Government ground, and that the remainder might be purchased cheap or exchanged for land in the Zuurveld, where the Dutch Boer would be more at home, and would most likely be glad to go if favourable terms were offered him.

His Excellency said, 'The Secretary of State would think me mad if I were to propose purchasing land, when nine-tenths of the Colony still belongs to the Government; and as to the dangers of the Zuurveld, the British nation is powerful enough to protect its settlers wherever it sends them.'

Stockenström openly criticised Governor Lord Charles Somerset's frontier policy. He also quarrelled with the Governor's son, Col Henry Somerset. The Graaff-Reinet district's contact with the frontier was diminished by the creation in 1821 of the separate district of Albany (out of Uitenhage) and in 1826 of the district of Somerset (later Somerset East, out of Graaff-Reinet). But Andries remained landdrost until the reform of 1828 which abolished that office.

Duminy writes:

> *Throughout his administrative career Stockenström accepted the broad principles of good government, but remained a fearless critic of many of the absurdities of policies framed in Cape Town or in London, and of the extravagant claims of the LMS.*

In 1828 Andries married Elsabe Helena Maasdorp (1808-1889), daughter of Gijsbert Henry Maasdorp. The couple had six children, of whom the firstborn died as a baby.

> *Early in 1829 Major-General Richard Bourke, who had arrived in the colony in 1826 as Lieutenant-Governor of the Eastern Province, but instead became Acting Governor when Lord Charles Somerset departed, appointed Andries to the new post of Commissioner-General for the Eastern Province.*

Duminy comments:

> *Andries became progressively more critical of frontier policy, both in his reports from Graaff-Reinet and in the deliberations of the Council of Advice. After Lord Stanley, Secretary for the Colonies, had requested his resignation from the council, Andries left the colony early in 1833 and, while in London, resigned as Commissioner-General. When news reached him of the outbreak in December 1834 of the Sixth Frontier War, he decided to settle in Sweden.*

Maj Gen Bourke

His career took a new turn after he gave evidence to the House of Commons select committee on aborigines in August 1835. His views, while critical of the philanthropists, impressed Lord Glenelg, the new Secretary for the Colonies, who appointed him Lieutenant-Governor of the Eastern Province. His tenure in this post was characterised by virulent and libellous campaigns against him, waged by Col Somerset, Godlonton and a variety of other interested parties, which served to nullify all the good he attempted to do in bringing peace to the frontier. He felt his position hopeless, and travelled to Britain to consult Glenelg who refused to accept Andries's resignation, but his successor, Lord Normanby, dismissed Andries anyway in August 1839.

As a reward for his service, Andries was created baronet a decade later in 1849, and given a pension of £700 a year.

Returning to the Cape in May 1840 he lived on his farm Klipkraal,[38] in the Swaershoek Valley near Somerset East; in Uitenhage and in Cape

---

38. Is this the original name of the farm currently owned by Richard Glennie, called Upsal, after Upsala in Sweden?

Town. In 1845 he settled on his farm Maasström at the foot of the Kaga Mountains.

When Representative Government was instituted in 1853, Sir Andries was approached to run for election to Parliament for the Eastern Divisions. To meet the expenses of the campaign he arranged for the subdivision of a part of Maasström as a township, which was named Bedford, after Sir Andries's friend, the 8th Duke of Bedford. Following a heated electoral campaign, Sir Andries defeated his old enemy, Godlonton – despite renewed publication of all the old accusations against him in the Graham's Town Journal – by almost 2 000 votes.

The 8th Duke of Bedford

Failing health saw him resign his seat in March 1856, and he left the colony the following month. He lived for a while in Nice, Naples and England, returned to the Cape in 1860, and again went to London in '62, where he eventually died of the bronchitis that had plagued him for years. He was buried in Kensel Green cemetery, London

Although he was constantly reviled by settlers for his perceived sympathies with the Xhosa, historian Christopher Saunders[39] described

---

39. Emeritus Professor of Historical Studies, University of Cape Town; editor at the *South Africa Historical Journal*

his legacy thus: 'No man in the 19th century Cape had greater breadth of vision, none gained the respect of a wider constituency, black as well as white.'

> *His public life was a continual protest against oppression and wrong in any shape, a constant struggle for true freedom. He was by nature a fighter. Nothing was more remarkable about him than his entire fearlessness. His indomitable courage, coupled with his natural pugnacity, led him at all periods of his public career into collision with those who differed from him, or pursued objects which he disapproved. That he should have made many enemies can excite no wonder.[40]*

---

40. Morris M, *Every Step Of The Way: The Journey To Freedom In South Africa*, South Africa: Ministry of Education - HSRC Press, 2004

7.

Lord Charles Somerset

The British occupation of the Cape

One of the several ways in which Lord Charles Somerset[41] differed from British Governors who preceded him was that from the beginning he created much more than a temporary home for himself and his family in South Africa. He identified himself more intimately with the life of the country, especially in the fields of sport and agriculture, than his predecessors and as a result developed a lasting attachment for it and a lifelong interest in its welfare.

At the time he assumed office, the Cape had reached a fresh phase in its history. There seemed little likelihood that Britain would willingly relinquish possession for a second time. Its strategic importance had become too patent in the course of the long struggle for, situated on the main sea route between Europe and the East, and midway across Britain's vital link with India, the Cape could not be allowed to remain

<hr>

41. Miller, Anthony Kendall, *Plantagenet in South Africa: Lord Charles Somerse*, Oxford University
Press 1965

a potential base for a hostile power: a British Admiral described the position in a phrase when he declared: 'What was a feather in the hands of Holland may become a sword in the hands of France'.

The first period of British occupation had ended in February 1803 when, under the Peace of Amiens, the newly created Batavian Republic of Holland assumed authority in place of the old Dutch East India Company which had finally been reduced to bankruptcy.

Millar writes:

> *Commissioner General Jacob Abraham de Mist, an able lawyer, and General Jan Willem Janssens, a distinguished soldier, were appointed to head the new Government of the Cape and at the same time reorganise and modernise the entire system of administration according to a plan prepared by De Mist. It embraced reforms, such as freedom of worship, which were part of the 'new order' introduced to Europe by Napoleon. It was a country of complex problems for a high-born English aristocrat to administer, especially one whose entire life had so far been spent in sophisticated society, at the focal point of powerful Empire. But it was a challenge to which Lord Charles responded with unbounded energy although he fretted under the irksome curb of the Colonial Office in London. To the inhabitants of the Colony it might seem as if the Governor was all-powerful for every act of legislation appeared under his name by Proclamation; in reality he was bound by many administrative regulations and instructions issued by the Colonial Office. Observance in the minutest detail was frequently demanded and expected and for this the Governor was answerable directly to the Minister of War and the Colonies. During the whole period of Lord Charles's Governorship, Earl Bathurst held this office, and all appointments of consequence in the administrative and judicial establishments required his official confirmation. At the same time the Governor was obliged to execute the policies of the British Government whether he agreed with them or not.*

The Governor's position, then, was neither a 'path of roses' nor a 'bed of down' but an exacting office demanding a high sense of duty and dedication.

In these respects Lord Charles was well equipped, for to his mind noblesse oblige was no mere phrase but an injunction sanctified by the honour of his family and the example of his ancestors. An excess of zeal and an impatient intolerance were faults indeed that often marred his achievements but no one would have ventured to accuse him of neglect or indolence, however tiresome and tedious the claims of office.

He had at his command clerks to compile the multifarious reports and despatches for London, but as any student of the period will discover, Lord Charles left little correspondence of consequence to his subordinates in his relations with the seat of Government in London. The stamp of his personality is unmistakable in the vivid literary style that marks the despatches sent from the Cape while he was Governor. And the *Records of the Cape Colony*, assembled by the historian George McCall Theal in more than thirty volumes, testify to the vast quantity of business transacted during his Governorship.

Lord Charles Somerset's first administrative acts were sound and

Simon's Bay naval base in 1806

sensible. He separated the naval establishment at Simons Town from the Cape District in May 1814, established an experimental farm at Boschberg on the Eastern Frontier for the primary purpose of tobacco growing, and developed Groote Post farm some forty miles north of Cape Town for the breeding of cattle, sheep and horses. A distinguished botanist, Dr Joseph Mackrill, was appointed as Superintendent at Boschberg, which was named Somerset farm, later to become the town of Somerset East. The tobacco-growing experiment was unsuccessful but the farm itself flourished and became an important factor in the development of the Eastern Cape as it was used to provide supplies needed by the military forces employed on the frontier.

Lord Charles was an enthusiastic and progressive agriculturist, and was never deterred by consideration for others from adopting what he considered to be the best policy. The Board of Agriculture offered him the Presidency of their venerable institution and he accepted with alacrity. But with himself as President he decided the board was redundant. He dissolved it forthwith and by doing so saved the Colony £350 a year in salaries.

The protection of wild life also engaged his interest. Finding that 'many idle and disorderly persons who ought to be dependent upon their industry wasted and misspent their time destroying game, particularly during the breeding season', he introduced by proclamation on 29 July 1814, a close season for game from August to December, but at the same time offered rewards to those who destroyed such noxious animals as 'tiger, wolf, and wild cat, mouse-hound and hawk'. The proclamation was substantially ignored as such caveats often are, and later in the year he felt compelled to prohibit the killing of game without a licence, and forbade entirely, the most immoral and profligate practice of employing the Sabbath day as a day particularly appropriate to the amusement of shooting such game as hare, zebras, partridges, pheasants, khorhaan, pauws, ostriches, and the whole antelope species'.

In his book[42] W.W. Bird wrote:

> *To be in disgrace at Government House is nearly to be banished from society; to offend the Governor is nearly to become an outlaw. No one dares to look at or to greet the individual who has incurred viceroyal displeasure; few venture to give opinions not consonant with those of the arbiter of wisdom, who presides over the fortunes of every member of the Colonial Community.*

The whole twelve years of Lord Charles Somerset's government forms one of the darkest parts of South African history, and fitly terminated with a recall to England which was tantamount to his dismissal for maladministration.

Pringle and Fairbairn found themselves ostracised by those fearful of the Governor, and a certain Cape Town clergyman was told that he was earning a reputation for himself of being one of the 'disaffected' because he had been observed still associating with Pringle and Fairbairn.

Lord Charles Somerset's attitude towards Pringle was quite as unreasonable and unrelenting as that of Pringle towards him. With Somerset, however, his prejudices extended themselves to Thomas's family. When Somerset Farm was closed as a Government institution Superintendent Hart and Thomas's brother John left to take up farming on their own properties. During Somerset's conciliatory visit to the frontier Hart approached him with a request for himself and his two assistants, Devenish and John Pringle, to retain in their service certain 'prize apprentices' until their indenture should expire. While granting permission to the first two men, Somerset asked, 'what claims John Pringle had to such a favour.' When Hart explained that Pringle had served the Government very well for four years, Somerset said he supposed that as soon as he was out of Government service he would, set himself to disturb and oppose constitutional authority like his brother Thomas ...'

---

42. *The State of the Cape of Good Hope in 1822*

A person who has done more mischief to the Government than any other in the Colony.'

Mr Hart expressed doubt that John Pringle would concern himself in such matters, adding that his education, at any rate, did not qualify him to meddle in literary or political matters. Somerset replied, 'So much the better! The less education the better! thus unconsciously expressing his own traditional views on the matter.'

(When John Pringle left his position as assistant-superintendent at Somerset Farm to live on his own farm at Glen Thorn, he was presented by Landdrost Stockenström with some sheep rams which formed the nucleus of the now well-established merino flock of Glen Thorn.)

8.

The Governor, the transvestite and the unbalanced 'libeller'

'A person, living at Newlands, makes it known, or takes this method of making it known, to the Public authorities of this Colony that on the 5th [May 1824] he detected Lord Charles buggering Dr Barry.'

This was the 'placard' affixed to the post of a wooden bridge on the Heerengracht that greeted the amazed eyes of a certain Captain John Findlay who resided in a cottage nearby.

Dr Barry,[43] in reality an Irish girl from Cork who assumed the name of her uncle, becoming a physician in the British army with service in many parts of the Empire. At the time, Dr Barry was Colonial Medical Inspector at the Cape but also family physician to Lord Charles Somerset, Governor of the Colony. The fascinating story of a woman taking extreme measures to work in a man's world has this account of a scandal that rocked the Cape:

It (the placard) was first observed by Thomas Kift Deane, secretary to the Colonial Medical Inspector, Dr James Barry. Mr Deane saw two slave boys and a man in a grey cloak looking at a notice on which he made out the words 'Barry' and 'Lord Charles'. When he went to the scene, the notice was gone.

The story gained traction when, later in the day, Deane encountered his neighbour, Captain Findlay, a sea captain, who told him he had come out onto his veranda at dawn and 'noticed some youths — one

43. *Dr James Barry, a Woman Ahead of her Time*, Michael du Preez & Jeremy Dronfield, Oneworld Publications, 2016

black, the other Asian — looking at a paper attached to the bridge post.' Findlay approached and 'could scarcely credit his senses' when he read what was written there. He returned to his house, 'having come out in his stockinged feet' but in the meantime an unknown horseman had removed the offending material. However, the contents 'spread through Cape Town with all the rapidity of the juiciest gossip.'

Samuel Eusebius Hudson, secretary to the previous Governor, Lord Macartney, wrote in his diary:

> *A most diabolical Placard has been stuck up accusing His Excellency Lord Charles Somerset with unnatural practices with Dr James Barry.*

He seemed both shocked and thrilled by this salacious rumour – if true, infamous, if false a malignant smear. But he showed his colours when referring to the Governor as 'this disgraceful man'. He was of the opinion that since Lord Charles's wife was at the end of a pregnancy, his 'proven appetites might turn elsewhere'. The bond between them could only be described as love.

Someone who shared Hudson's opinion of Lord Charles was William Wilberforce Bird, a cousin of the philanthropist William Wilberforce, with whom he shared an interest in the well-being of slaves. He arrived at the Cape of Good Hope, South Africa, in 1807 where he founded the Cape Philanthropic Society. In 1810, he was appointed Controller of Customs, a civil service position he retained until his death. In a controversial book Bird[44] wrote:

> *To be in disgrace at Government House is nearly to be banished from society; to offend the Governor is nearly to become an outlaw. No one dares to look at or to greet the individual who has incurred vice-royal displeasure; few venture to give opinions not consonant with those of the arbiter of wisdom, who presides over the fortunes of every member of the Colonial Community.*

---

44. *The State of the Cape of Good Hope in 1822*, WW Bird, John Murray, 1823

Within three days the Fiscal, Daniel Denyssen, launched a court of inquiry into what had become known as 'the Placard' (plakaat in Dutch), the effect of which had been, in the Fiscal's words, 'to wound the heart of Lord Charles' and 'to create the most abominable suspicions in the hearts of the inhabitants'.

With the breath of conspiracy in the air, three suspects were summoned to the enquiry. The first was printer and newspaper proprietor George Greig, a Scotsman recently arrived in Cape Town who the previous year had been given permission to set up a newspaper to rival the government-backed *Cape Town Gazette* and *African Advertiser*. Mr Greig's *South African Commercial Advertiser* was a much more sensational organ that instantly upset the government with its political radicalism, allegedly misreporting trials, among other scurrilous practices. In May, the Fiscal had formally gagged the *Commercial Advertiser* and shut it down on grounds of 'deviation from the prospectus' originally submitted by Greig.

The second possible conspirator was Greig's clerk, Joseph Green, while the third was a much shadier character. William Edwards was an Englishman, also recently arrived at the Cape. He had set up as a notary and lawyer and within weeks had become a stone in the boot of the government. He continuously brought frivolous libel cases against the Governor and the Fiscal, and acquired a reputation for aggressiveness and showmanship in court, with interminable addresses which drew large crowds. Edwards himself had been variously charged with libel and contempt of court, and upon investigation had been proved a fraud with no qualifications whatsoever to practise law – the closest he had come to certification had been working in Chester as a prothonotary (principal clerk of a court) and marrying his principal's daughter. By March 1824 he was awaiting trial and repeatedly bothering Lord Charles and Earl Bathurst with letters complaining about his mistreatment while on remand in the Tronk (in fact he lived quite comfortably thanks to his wealth, and wasn't subject to the privations of the other prisoners). His trial had occurred in May; he was sentenced to transportation to New South Wales and was now appealing against his conviction.

William Edwards was clearly unbalanced, dishonest, and had an addiction to perceiving and perpetrating libels involving Lord Charles. One of the black marks against George Greig was his sympathetic reporting of Edwards's trial. This was enough to convince the Fiscal that Greig and Edwards were responsible for the Placard. Undoubtedly they had a proven record of anti-government libel, but then again they were the very men the Fiscal wanted to pin a crime upon, and he needed a quick resolution.

A fourth conspirator was added to the picture — a man with the unusual name of Bishop Burnett, a former naval lieutenant turned farmer with a record of wild, violent behaviour and a vicious temper. He came into the picture at the public inquiry when William Edwards's servant, Daniel Lee, was put on the stand. He confessed that in May he had delivered a package of papers from Burnett to his master; upon receiving it, Edwards opened it, took out the Placard and read it, and, 'he laughed so loudly as to make me take particular notice of what he read'. He cast some doubt on his reliability as a witness by referring to the libel as, 'concerning Lord Charles and Dr Barry's wife', but it was seen as strong evidence against Edwards.

The homes of the suspects were thoroughly searched, but apart from a few satirical notes, no evidence of their guilt — or even complicity — could be found. And despite the succession of closely questioned witnesses, no conclusive evidence was uncovered. With deep regret, the Fiscal marked the case unsolved and hoped that more evidence would come to light in the future.

It did not. The author of the Placard was never identified with certainty, and it became part of the minutiae of Cape folklore. And yet there were many questions never asked — let alone answered — by the inquiry. One was the peculiar wording of the Placard, particularly its central claim —

that a witness 'detected Lord Charles buggering Dr Barry'. That coarse term would be an odd choice for literate men such as Burnett, Greig and Edwards, who were passably educated and keenly interested in the law. Surely they would more likely have written 'sodomising', which was not only a more literate expression but also a legal term (denoting an act that in the armed forces was punishable by death). The word sat strangely with the otherwise legalistic phrasing ('A person, living at Newlands, makes it known, or takes this method of making it known, to the Public authorities of this Colony'). It might well be taken that this was a genuine witness claim written down verbatim and embedded in legal phrasing.

Another question: if this was a calculated libel against the Governor, why didn't Greig, who had the equipment to hand, print up dozens of copies and, instead of flimsily wafering one to a bridge post, paste them to walls around the town, or scatter them about as handbills? And who was it that removed the Placard, and why? Thomas Deane's man in a grey cloak and Captain Findlay's horseman were never identified. The cloaked man had apparently crossed the bridge in the direction of the parade ground after looking at the Placard, so shortly before its disappearance that he must have taken it (unless the two slaves were responsible). Findlay's rider crossed the bridge from the parade ground (so might have met the cloaked man) arriving at a gallop and then riding away south, towards the centre of town.

Even if Burnett did originally pass the Placard to Edwards, was he or Greig necessarily the author? Possession did not prove authorship; it might be stolen property. Burnett himself appeared outraged at being implicated, and published a lengthy denial of the allegations against him — including Daniel Lee's claim to have passed the Placard from him to Edwards, which he called 'one monstrous falsehood', adding: 'What is meant by Doctor Barry's wife is best known to the conspirators, as he is, ever has been, and, if rumour speaks truth, ever will keep single.' This comment alone indicates that while Burnett knew the gossip about Dr

Barry's gender, he wasn't very familiar with the actual content of the Placard (which of course alleged a sexual act between Lord Charles and James, not James's non-existent wife). He claimed to have first heard of the Placard at the same time as the rest of Cape Town.

The scandalous incident at Newlands that the Placard claimed to report coincided with Lord Charles's residence there and Dr Barry's frequent presence in the weeks after the birth of the Somerset's new child. It fitted uncomfortably well. A stray fact, which may or may not be relevant, is that the incident was alleged to have occurred on Wednesday 5 May, the day before James was returned to full pay — a step probably assisted by Lord Charles's influence.

All this leads to an ultimate question. When James broke down in front of the shopkeeper's wife on the morning of the Placard's appearance, was it the distress of an innocent person slandered or of a guilty one exposed? And a further observation: if a witness really did see Lord Charles in the full act of adultery, was it not strange that they didn't simultaneously discover that Dr Barry was a woman? Of course, that could depend on many things — not least the witness's viewpoint and the couple's state of undress and position of the guilty couple. Catching a fleeting glimpse of physical lovemaking in *flagrante delicto* between two people believed to be male, one might simply assume it to be homosexual.

If the allegation was a lie, it was peculiarly well chosen and well timed. As Samuel Hudson indicated, But love of what kind?

Clearly it was of a deep, sincere and durable kind. In Lord Charles's place, many men would have saved their own skin by putting up a defensive show of unity with their wife and publicly shunning Dr Barry. On the contrary, Lord Charles stood by James, even at the risk to his own reputation, with the steadfastness of real love.

Anthony Millar wrote:[45]

45. *Plantagenet in South Africa: Lord Charles Somerset*, Anthony Kendall Millar, Oxford University Press 1965

One of the several ways in which Lord Charles Somerset differed from British Governors who preceded him was that from the beginning he created much more than a temporary home for himself and his family in South Africa. He identified himself more intimately with the life of the country, especially in the fields of sport and agriculture, than his predecessors and as a result developed a lasting attachment for it and a lifelong interest in its welfare.

His eldest son, Henry, who later joined him at the Cape and served for decades as Commandant of the Eastern Frontier, left descendants on African soil so that Lord Charles also has the distinction of being the progenitor of more citizens of the present day Republic of South Africa than any other British Governor.

'A most diabolical Placard has been stuck up accusing His Excellency Lord Charles Somerset with unnatural practices with Dr Barry,' wrote Cape Town resident Samuel Eusebius Hudson[46], his scratchy nib racing eagerly, scarcely legibly, across the page of his diary; 'it has thrown the whole Cape into consternation. If true, it is pregnant with infamy to the parties. If false, it is a most convincing proof of what length the malignant will go to smear the character of this disgraceful man. 'How galling it must be to the friends of Lord Charles and Dr Barry,' Hudson went on, torn between glee and impartiality; 'There are many who will enjoy to see these Arrogants humbled but if innocent the scheme is a diabolical one.'

Large rewards for the apprehension of the culprit were offered - 6 000 rix dollars by Lord Charles, 1 000 by Dr Barry (a hefty portion of his annual salary) and 14 000 by a subscription from the town's merchant class.

Pringle and Fairbairn found themselves ostracised by those fearful of the Governor, and a certain Cape Town clergyman was told that he was earning a reputation for himself of being one of the 'disaffected'

---

46. Samuel Hudson had come out from England in 1796 on the staff of Lord Macartney, the first Governor, and had found all the subsequent governors wanting

because he had been observed still associating with Pringle and Fairbairn.

Lord Charles Somerset's attitude towards Pringle was quite as unreasonable and unrelenting as that of Pringle towards him.

9.

Grahamstown

Sir John Cradock

Sir John Cradock decided that the whole of the Cape Regiment should remain permanently stationed in the Zuurveld, and instructed Colonel Graham to select for the military headquarters some suitable spot which also should admit of a number of settlers establishing themselves on it. On 3 May Colonel Graham chose the old farm *Noutoe*, now Table Farm, which had been abandoned and the Cape Regiment was moved there. As adjutant of the regiment Hart retained this post until it was disbanded, serving mostly along the borders of the Eastern Cape.

Table Farm was occupied by Major Thomas Charles White[47] who brought out his own party in 1820, chartering the ship *Stentor* which sailed from Liverpool on 13 January and arrived in Table Bay on 19 April, where the charter terminated. They were to be located at what is now known as Riviers-Sonder-End, 70 miles from Cape Town. It is not clear why this site was chosen as it was not in the remit of the Settlers scheme. In the event, Thomas White refused the location and the party

---

47. Francis White, great-grandson of Thomas Charles White, undertook extensive research for a privately published family history

was relocated to Albany and boarded the *Sir George Osborne* for Algoa Bay. We have a record of some interesting correspondence between the Major and the Agent for Transports, Lieut Charles Church RN. These letters were accessed from the National Archives in Kew. He had been advised of the regulations which stated that:

> *The Settlers are not to be allowed to embark arms or gunpowder without an order from the Secretary of State for which it is requisite that they should apply. No dogs are to be embarked unless the parties obtain an order from the Secretary of State for the purpose, and in that case they must put on board water for them for 84 days at their own expense.*

Writing from his home, Mount Pleasant, in Liverpool on 20 December 1819, Thomas requested permission to take his dogs.

> *I beg leave to request you will have the goodness to allow me to take 2 Greyhounds and 2 Spaniels on board the ship Stentor. I have not only provided Water and Provisions for the Voyage, but have also procured Crates, in which the dogs would be confined when not taking exercise by permission of the Master.*

Thomas White lost his life in the 6th Frontier War - Hintsa's War (1834 -1835) in which he served as a Major in the Grahamstown Volunteers.

Robert Hart has another claim to fame – that of selecting the site of Grahamstown. Because of his intimate knowledge of that part of the country, Hart was asked by Colonel Graham to select a suitable place for the establishment of the military headquarters.[48]

Hart chose the site where Grahamstown[49] now stands and built one of the first houses there for himself and his family. In his

48. Talk by Mrs. Doris Craib at the Somerset East Museum's Annual General Meeting in March 1977

49. To the embryo town thus formed a name was officially sanctioned on 14 August 1812 by the following Government advertisement: 'His Excellency the Governor and Commander in Chief is pleased to notify and direct that the present Head-quarter Cantonment of the Cape Regiment, situated in the Zuure Veld, which is also to be the future Residence of the Deputy Landdrost of Uitenhage, shall be henceforward designated and only acknowledged, by the name of Graham's Town, in testimony of His Excellency's Respect for the Services of Lieutenant-Colonel Graham, through whose able exertions the Kaffer Tribes have been expelled from that valuable District.'

Early view of Grahamstown

spare time he indulged his life-long interest in agriculture. Working his plot in a small way he soon had a flourishing garden and was able to supplement his army pay by the sale of vegetables. When Colonel Graham decided to establish a village there, Hart's plot was found to be in the way of a planned street. So instead he was given a plot of land in Belmont Valley which was called 'Sunnyside'.

Grahamstown, which up to this time was little more than a name, and consisted simply of the camp of the few officers and men of the Cape Regiment who were not on outpost duty, was thus in possession of an administrative organisation. The next step towards the formation of the prospective town was to attract civilian settlers. To this end there was suggested, in the first place, an indefinite scheme of granting, at small cost, plots of land for building purposes.

There was some controversy as to whether Hart or Andries Stockenström selected the site of the town. Carol Tarr wrote:

I was interested to read Mr CC Wiles' letter headed 'Man Who selected Site of Grahamstown', which appeared in your edition of September 9th and which named Andries Stockenström the younger as the selector of the site of our city. There seems to be a certain amount of discrepancy on the subject. In your issue of the 4th the credit is given to Stockenström, whose claim is supported by Mr. Wiles and also who wrote to the 'Herald' on the subject about a year ago.

Sir James Rose-Innes, however, in his excellent autobiography describes his ancestor Robert Hart as the one who selected this post for the military headquarters of the Eastern Border. I have in my possession a copy of an excerpt from the Somerset and Bedford Courant dated Saturday, September 21st, 1867, which contains Robert Hart's obituary. It is clear from this extract that Robert Hart as adjutant was requested by Colonel Graham to select the site of Grahamstown, and it is unlikely that Hart would have delegated this task to Ensign Andries Stockenström.[50]

Grahamstown was the centre of the newly-created district of Albany which was defined as that portion of the district of Uitenhage which hitherto had been known as the Zuurveld. Metrowitch[51] wrote:

Graham's Tree in High Street, as the mimosa was named, was well cared for by the early inhabitants who appreciated its historical significance, and it became a favourite meeting place for the citizens. Often on hot summer evenings they would sit in its shade and point with pride to the nail in its trunk on which the gallant colonel was reputed to have hung his sword. The tree grew to an immense size but about thirty years later it was blown down in a violent gale. A large, hideous, stone water-tank built in a style known as 'Hottentot Gothic' was subsequently erected on the site where it had stood, but, as the place became the favourite haunt of all the vagrants in the town, it had to be removed. For over sixty years the spot remained unmarked and then in 1912, during the centenary celebrations of the city, the present simple dignified monument was erected with an inscription on its east face reading:

---

50. Letter to the Editor, *Grocott's Daily Mail*, 12 Sep 1952: *Responsible For Selecting The Site Of Grahamstown*. From Carol Tarr

51. Metrowich, FC, *The Valiant But Once*, Howard Timmins 1974

'On This Spot stood the tree under which Lieut. Col. Graham and Capt Stockenström decided upon the present site of the City Of Grahamstown in June 1812.'

By a strange twist of fate, Grahamstown, baptised in the blood and strife of a fierce frontier struggle and nurtured on the turbulent fire of incessant cruel warfare, is today a mellow, peaceful cathedral city and one of the main seats of culture in South Africa.

Early in 1813, Sir John Cradock applied for permission to resign his governorship of the Colony. On October 13th, Earl Bathurst replied, stating that HRH the Prince Regent had accepted the resignation, and expressed his high sense of the services Sir John Cradock had rendered to the Colony during his term of office, and regretted that he (Cradock) had found it necessary to withdraw from the inhabitants of the settlement 'a superintendence in which you have shown so much assiduity, judgment and ability, and which has been uniformly exercised with a view to their advancement in happiness and prosperity.'

His successor was Lord Charles Henry Somerset, who was appointed by Royal Commission, dated November 2nd, 1813.

1820 Settlers

Ivan Mitford- Barberton's sculpture of an 1820 Settler Family

10.

The 1820 Settlers

Ben Maclennan has written several books, including *The wind makes Dust*, an anthology of four hundred years of the history of the Cape from the early European settlers to the present day. In his book on John Graham[52] he writes:

> *The 1820 settlers, some of whom had arrived at Algoa expecting to find apricots growing wild in the thorn bush, soon discovered how brash Somerset's words about the new land had been. There were the inevitable Xhosa raids; the locations were too small for cattle farming and unsuitable for growing crops; they experienced both drought and floods which, in October 1823, 'swept away much of the produce of the best available lands', and disease, which destroyed three successive wheat crops.*
>
> *Many flocked to the towns where they found outlets for their skills. Others, after the government belatedly realised its folly and in 1825 enlarged the grants of land, began to breed merino and other types of woolled sheep on a large scale. Not least among the reasons for the popularity of this type of farming was the belief that since the Xhosa were not themselves sheep farmers, they would seldom steal more than the odd one for food.*

Another writer, Dorothy Rivett-Carnac[53], recorded the dreadful weather conditions:

---

52. *A Proper Degree of Terror, John Graham and the Cape's Eastern Frontier*, Ben Maclennan, Ravan Press, Johannesburg

53. *Thus Came the English in 1820*, Dorothy Rivett-Carnac, Howard Timmins, Cape Town, 1961

A prolonged drought was followed by torrential rains with violent squalls of wind which did great damage to the farms and the little villages established by the settlers. Gardens and fences were swept away and whole crops disappeared. The fragile wood-and-mud houses were destroyed by destructive gales or by the raging torrents which took the place of the docile streams on whose banks the settlers had built. Too late, they recollected the advice of Robert Hart, manager of Somerset Farm, 'to build always on the side of a hill facing the rising sun.' To the desolate scene was added a plague of locusts and an infestation of grubs which devoured the last vestiges of vegetation on their pathetic plots. There seemed no end to the sequence of disaster.

In evidence to those who sought to help them, the settlers recounted experiences which only exceptional courage enabled them to survive. 'My wheat, two months ago the most promising I ever saw in any country, is now cut in heaps for burning: the rust utterly destroyed it,' one settler testified, 'My barley, from the drought and grub which attacked the blade, produced little more than I sowed. My Indian corn very much injured by the caterpillar: cabbages destroyed by the lice: carrots run to seed: the potatoes are good but I have but a small quantity. Our cows are dry from want of grass … On Saturday, when watching by the sick bed of my little girl, stung by a reptile, I was startled by the cry of wild dogs and saw about thirty of those ferocious animals who killed twenty of my flock of twenty-seven before I could drive them off.'

11.

Somerset Farm

The Boschberg

Somerset Farm[54] owed its origin to a somewhat remote cause – the severe financial depression in England owing to the Napoleonic Wars. The revenue of the Colony not being adequate to meet its expenditure, the Governor was instructed to exercise the most rigid economy. One of his schemes for increasing the revenue was to grow tobacco for export.

There was in Cape Town at this time a Dr Mackrill, an enthusiastic botanist, who not long previously had arrived from America and who seemed to be a man eminently capable of furthering the governor's views. He was instructed to make a tour of the East for the purpose of investigating the possibilities of the country, and, if a suitable spot were discovered, of conducting experiments in connection with the growth of tobacco and agricultural development generally. His investigations led to the area around Boschberg on the eastern frontier. Here Willem

---

54. SMD 114/2b „SM". undated article (ca 1970). *Robert Hart of Glen Avon; A Friend of the Settlers*, typescript 'written for 1820 Centenary'. Donor: Mrs E Armstrong. Repository: Albany Museum (History), Grahamstown

Prinsloo, an old elephant hunter had leased part of his property to Louis Trichardt[55] and an adjoining portion to one Bester.

In reporting on these Mackrill wrote:

> *The approach to the farm is over a lawn seven miles wide and God knows how long, comprising at least a thousand acres of level rich land, clear as a park and covered with excellent sweet pasture. Arrived at the Boschberg, you view with delight the beauty of this mountain which bound the north side of the farm; it has not an inch of useless ground, being covered with grass and timber to the summit. The arable part of the estate consists of two valleys of great extent and fertility; more than a thousand acres submit without trouble to irrigation, and by good management of the water-courses, leading them over the sides of gently rising hills, arable land can be had to almost any extent.*

No doubt Mackrill was impressed by the success if Trichardt's enterprise – 6 000 tobacco plants, two well-stocked vegetable gardens and 30 wagon-loads of pumpkins - expropriated the property in 1814 (with the payment 200 rix dollars[56]).

Dr Mackrill was put in charge of the project and took possession on New Year's Day 1815 with his family and dependants, numbering twenty in all. On Dr Mackrill's suggestion to Lord Charles Somerset 'that the land merits Your Excellency's noble and ancient name,' the farm was called the   Somerset Farm. He immediately took over the farming operations and to grow whatever he could to supply the troops on the frontier. He also set to work to build accommodation for the soldiers, white and coloured, that were to be stationed there.

However, with no business experience or practical knowledge he was

---

55. Trichardt, born in 1783, was educated at Graaff Reinet and after his marriage started farming tobacco and other crops at Boschberg. Trichardt then moved to Albany and from there, in 1833, led a party of family and friends on trek, perhaps harbouring further resentment towards the interference of authority

56. In 1781 Governor Van Plettenberg issued paper bank notes worth almost 100 000 rijksdaalders (rix dollars). The rix dollar was originally a silver coin issued in the Netherlands but used as currency in many countries. By 1825, the rix dollar's value was fixed at 1 shilling 6 pence

unable to make a success of the tobacco project. Nor was he able to produce sufficient potatoes, pumpkins and other vegetable to supply the forces and supplementary harvest had to be purchased from the farmers. These farmers had previously sold their crops directly to the troops, and although they were more than willing to sell to Somerset Farm they soon found that the prices paid them provided for a large profit being made for the Government. They refused to sell to the farm, and were paid scant attention to the Proclamation by His Excellency that anyone who put obstacles in the way of the smooth working of the farm would be severely dealt with.

Things went from bad to worse. Disaffection spread from the farmers to the dependents of the farm itself. When the baker struck, the Hottentot soldiers refused to work. The military authorities declined to interfere on the grounds that the soldiers were employed on the farm in a civilian capacity but they refused to acknowledge the Superintendent's authority. Mackrill, in a report to the Government, wrote:

> *All the influence I formerly possessed over the soldiery is totally vanished, and every man does as he pleases, knowing they have no punishment to fear.*

Not long after, in April 1816, he appealed to Lord Charles Somerset to be relieved of his charge:

> *I am, my lord, growing old very fast and do not possess that activity which is so indispensable for the promotion of your Excellency's views.*

This is when Hart took over. He certainly increased production on the farm, supplying not only the soldiers but many of the settlers too. The farm was financed by the Colonial Government and the supplies to the troops and settlers were paid by the Imperial Government, often at an advance of 100 per cent. This was reminiscent of the state of affairs between the Dutch East India Company and the farmers in the Cape more than a century earlier. Somerset was clearly on the make and it is known that the drostdies in Grahamstown and Bathurst were built with profits from the Somerset farm. No profits found their way to Robert Hart, who simply carried out the instructions of an autocratic superior and was constantly making piteous appeals for his salary.

Lord Charles Somerset made his first visit to the frontier on 27 January 1817, accompanied by his two daughters, the Colonial Secretary, Colonel Bird, Mr Thomas Sheridan and the famous Dr Barry.[57]

Despite the reduction of the military protection on the border, the success of Somerset farm from 1817 to 1825 under the supervision of Hart was not less than spectacular[58]. He made it a model for the whole Cape frontier. He brought 600 acres under cultivation - a vast area in those days. He demonstrated the first up-to-date farm machinery for grinding wheat ever seen in that wild region, only a dozen miles from Kaffirland. The machinery was shipped out from Scotland and then transported by ox wagon from Algoa Bay over the Zuurberg Pass. The mill could produce two tons of meal a day and soon Robert was grinding all the wheat grown between Pearston, Ann's Villa and Zwagershoek.

In his new post at the Boschberg, Hart took part in the astounding transformation of the Zuurveld. From having been the most dangerous and savage part of the Cape Colony it became the most closely settled and progressive - a civilizing centre on the very border of the Bantu country. On the Government's behalf he supplied rations to the entire frontier garrison from the sea to Cradock, buying large additional stocks of wheat and slaughter animals from the frontier Boers. He thus gave them the first orderly, convenient marketing they had ever enjoyed. Since money was meaningless on the frontier he secured shipments twice a year through Algoa Bay of the goods the Boers wanted most. Travellers

---

57. Dr Barry had been appointed assistant surgeon to the army in 1815 and took up his position in the Cape the following year

58. From the series *They Were South Africans*, a broadcast on the English Transmission by journalist and historian, John Bond and published in the SABC magazine on 19 July 1954

remarked with amazement that on this bustling farm the very Hottentots seemed to acquire the energy of tireless Robert Hart.

Algoa Bay

Algoa Bay, where ships had hitherto called only two or three times a year to supply Captain Evatt and his men at Fort Frederick, became at a bound the second port of South Africa. Through it the civilizing contacts and influences of Europe reached out to the Cape frontier and far beyond. Hart must have met all the future Voortrekker leaders while buying corn, cattle and sheep for the Somerset Farm military depot from 1817 onwards. He was a close friend of Piet Retief. He lived to see Port Elizabeth become, with Grahamstown, the trading base of the Free State and Transvaal Voortrekkers.

The only Scottish party among the 1820 Settlers passed close to the Somerset Farm on the way to their dangerously isolated destination on the Baviaans River. Hart heard of their coming and went out to guide them to their future home in person. Thomas Pringle wrote that, for all his stern and austere exterior, Major Hart almost broke down when he heard the voices of the Scottish women. Long-submerged memories of his mother and the home he had run away from in Scotland swept uncontrollably over him. Hart gave these Scottish settlers their first fruit-trees at the Baviaans River. He took Thomas Pringle on a memorable journey through the lichen-hung forests of the frontier, where elephants swarmed. He appointed Pringle's brother John as his assistant when hard times came - as they did very early - upon the 1820 Settlers. During their first hungry years in the Zuurveld, when rust wiped out their wheat, Hart supplied the settlers as well as the military with rations. This must have taxed the 600 acres he cultivated on Somerset Farm, as well as the supply system he had arranged with the scattered Voortrekkers-to-be.

Elephants in Addo

Hart's Scottish thrift and organizing ability made Somerset Farm one of the most profitable government undertakings in South Africa. The first big test for the Somerset Farm came in 1819, when the AmaXhosa tribes stormed down on Grahamstown itself in a desperate attempt to recapture the Zuurveld. A still bigger test was to come a year later when Hart had to start supplying the 1820 settlers, as well as the troops, with rations. Without Somerset Farm many of the settlers might have perished of hunger in their first disastrous years of blight and flood.

Through hard work and great insight he soon made his farm a landmark in the region.[59] He bred top merino sheep, a breed introduced to South Africa by Colonel Graham, and so contributed greatly to what became an important industry. His orchards produced a fantastic bounty

---

59. *Country Life*, March 2000

of fruits, especially citrus, and his flood-irrigated fields delivered huge harvests of grain that soon justified a private mill.

Lord Charles Somerset ploughed back the profits into other development work in the Colony without obtaining the sanction of Whitehall. This was at a time when the financial condition of England necessitated the most rigid economy in connection with the distant Colonies. Further, Lord Charles Somerset's administration had already been the subject of adverse comment in England. Political opponents had drawn invidious comparisons between the expenditure at the Cape under the Batavian with that under Lord Charles Somerset's government. *The Morning Chronicle* of 19 December 1816 had severely criticised him, in what he called, 'a most scurrilous and at the same time contemptible and ignorant attack', in relation to the expense he was incurring for the improvement of the breed of horses and sheep.

Somerset was on the defensive, and with the attention which was thus drawn to the affairs of the Cape he was obliged to reduce expenditure; and one of his reactions was to downsize the garrison stationed there. But it was an ill-considered decision in view of the continuing conflict on the frontier. Almost before the military stations along the Fish River were properly established, orders were received (June, 1817) for the withdrawal of the 21st Light Dragoons and their transportation to India. In this same month also the Cape Regiment was to have been disbanded, but this was postponed until 24 September when, in its place a new Colonial corps - the Cape Corps - was formed.

The arrival of a commission of inquiry into South African affairs alarmed the doughty Governor. In a knee-jerk reaction, he decided to close Somerset Farm. Hart's reward for the success he had achieved was therefore a terse note on 7 January 1825, warning him to wind up the farm and dismiss all the staff, including himself, by the end of January.

George Cory

According to the historian, George Cory:[60]

The closing of the farm took place very suddenly owing to the allegations against him in a petition to the House of Commons. Lord Charles was recalled to England to defend himself but resigned before the case came on. Besides monopolising the military market, it furnished the greater quantity of rations to the settlers of 1820 during the first two or three years. The manner of carrying on the business became a scandal and formed one of the accusations against Lord Charles Somerset in a petition which was brought before the House of Commons. It appeared that the farm was financed by the Colonial Government, while the supplies to the troops were paid for by the Home Government. And as large profits were made by the farm, money passed from the Home Government to the Colonial in a manner which was not suspected by the Lords of the Treasury. In 1824, when it was announced that Commissioners of Inquiry were being sent out to investigate the real state of the Colony, and the several allegations against Lord Charles Somerset, the farm was suddenly closed down and the lands were formed into a township — the present town of Somerset East.

---

60. Vol 1 of GE Cory's *Rise of South Africa*

Hart was without a job after nearly thirty years' work of the strictest integrity for South Africa. Fortunately he had been granted land on an adjoining property[61] which he called Glen Avon. With the help of a small pension he was now able to start farming for himself.

Hart's new home became a great meeting-place in peace as in war. Missionaries from Kaffirland or the far-off 'Bootchuana country' were as welcome as visitors from Europe or farmers from far and wide. He made it one of the finest homesteads on the frontier, planted a vineyard, and established a notable orchard of orange and lemon trees. His two sons helped with the farming. His daughters (there were six but two died young) set many hearts beating faster among lonely young officers and settlers on the frontier. John Pringle, who had been his assistant on the Somerset Farm, became his son-in-law; so did his fellow-officer in the Cape Regiment, Charles Lennox Stretch.[62]

Stretch could tell stirring stories of the Battle of Grahamstown, which Hart had missed on Somerset Farm. But the anxieties of war were seldom entirely forgotten. In each succeeding Kaffir War—the war of 1834-5, the War of the Axe, and Umlanjeni's War of 1850-3—Glen Avon opened its doors to the homeless and the imperilled, fed them and protected them, just as the Somerset Farm no doubt did in 1819.

During Umlanjeni's War, the worst and last of the six that had surged around Hart and his family on the frontier, the farmers of Somerset East, English-speaking and Afrikaans-speaking alike, met to warn the government that they could endure these never-ending dangers and losses no longer. They elected Hart to the chair as the unquestioned head of the district and sent the government a warning that they would have to trek west to safer regions. Many did trek. Robert Hart, deep in his seventies now, was not among them.

---

61. The property was granted to him in 1817, probably as an incentive to leave Grahamstown and take over the Somerset where his salary was a pittance; he must have been comfortably settled in Grahamstown at the time

62. *Black Drift* by C Lennox Stretch

Soon he was one of the most successful pioneers of merino sheep-farming in the Eastern Cape, helping to establish South Africa's first major export. Following his example, the settlers began to breed merino and other types of woolled sheep on a large scale. Not least among the reasons for the popularity of this type of farming was the belief that since the Xhosa were not themselves sheep farmers, they would seldom steal more than the odd one for food.

A decade later the weight of export wool from the eastern districts alone was more than one hundred thousand pounds; and Thomas Pringle could write that 'there are about twelve thousand fine-woolled sheep in Albany, the owners of which are realising large profits; this promises to prove a mine of inexhaustible wealth for South Africa'. By 1842, the wool clip from the eastern districts was estimated at about a million pounds weight, valued at thirty-four thousand one hundred and fifty pounds, while the clip for the whole colony approached a million and a half pounds.

Albany was now boasting some two hundred thousand woolled sheep, the Cradock district was celebrated for the fatness of its stock and the opulence of its farmers, and Bruintjies Hoogte and the land along the Baviaans were reckoned to have some of the largest and most valuable

Merino ram

flocks in the colony. Further to the north, in what had once been the most remote and untamed part of the frontier, a wealthy Boer could offer his guests a meal of stewed fruit, meat, pastry, pickles and salads, served with silver spoons on plates of china and English Delft, with napkins.

Cape wool, without approaching the volume exported from Australia, nevertheless gained a significant foothold in the expanding British market - enough of a foothold to enable it to become the most important of the colony's farming activities, bringing new prosperity to the frontier districts and ensuring that the hills and valleys of the Zuurveld, once filled with human voices and the lowing of cattle, would for generations to come echo nothing more than the mindless bleating of thousands upon thousands of sheep.

'The day was when our plains were covered with tens of thousands of springboks,' wrote John Mitford Bowker,[63] one of the pioneer wool farmers of the frontier, in the 1840s. 'They are gone now, and who regrets it? Their place is occupied with tens of thousands of merino sheep: are they not better than the springbuck? Yet I must own that when I see two or three of them on the wide plains, and know they are the last of their race, my heart yearns towards them, and I regret that so much innocent beauty, elegance and agility must needs be swept from the earth.'

Charles Webb[64] disputed the claim that Hart was the first to introduce merino sheep to the area.

He wrote:

I saw in the obituary of that excellent colonist and good man, Mr Hart Snr of Somerset, a statement that, on the return of Lord Charles Somerset to the colony at the end of 1821, he finding some Merino sheep at Cape Town, sent them up to Mr Hart, at Somerset, and that he was the first person who introduced the Merinos into the Eastern Province. There is some mistake

---

63. *Bowkers of Tharfield* by Ivan Mitford-Barberton

64. Letter by Charles Webb Son, 16 Nov 1867, to the Graham's Town Journal (From *The Journals of Sophia Pigot*, 1819-1821, edited by Margaret Rainier, AA Balkema, Cape Town 1974

here, although, in claiming that honour for another, I hope the consequence will not be of much moment to the colony, or cause an earthquake. With all due respect to the memory of Mr Hart, I must claim that honour for Major George Pigot of Pigot Park. After the Major had brought up his party and family, and got into some kind of shelter, he sent two men down to the Bay to bring up two fine bulls, a Devon and a Fatherland, and the Devon was admired by all the country round. With the bulls were brought up, also, four noble-looking Merino rams and two ewes, one of them being the lamb of the other, and about 9 months old. These were placed under my charge in August or September, 1820, and I recollect Mr. Hart, as well as other gentlemen, coming to see them. Lord Charles did not leave England until nearly a year after, and the little Merinos were dancing about the hills at Pigot Park, long before he had left home to return to his Government. The sheep throve well and rapidly increased.

Thomas Pringle, in his Narrative tells of his meeting with Robert Hart:

A numerous party of us were assembled at tea in the officers' dining hall when Mr Hart joined us. The Scottish accent, seldom entirely lost even by the most polished of the middle ranks of our countrymen, was heard from every tongue, and the broad Doric dialect prevailed, spoken by female voices, fresh and unsophisticated from the banks of the Teviot and the fields of Lothain. Hart, a man of iron look and rigid nerve, was taken by surprise and deeply affected. The accents of his native tongue uttered by the kindly voice of women carried him back forty years at once and irresistibly, as he afterwards owned, to the scenes of his mother's fireside; and recalled freshly before him the softened remembrance of early life — those tender and sacred remembrances which, though apparently buried beneath the cares and ambitions of after-years, are never in any good heart entirely effaced.

He was known as 'Robert Hart the First', his elder son 'Robert Hart the Second'. Of his daughters, one married Lieut EL Stretch, another became Mrs Dodds Pringle of Lynedoch, a third married Robert Bowker of 'Craigie Burn' while the fourth was the wife of Mr Fleischer who died leaving her with two little girls. One of them became Mrs Rose-Innes, mother of an ex-Chief Justice and the other Mrs Gordon (afterwards Lady Sprigg). It is interesting to note how the Settler families inter-married, especially the Scottish ones, who have certainly kept up their reputation for clannishness.

Robert Hart junior

Vast herds of Springbok

The Zuurberg

12.

Thomas Pringle

Thomas Pringle[65] writes:

> *The following day, passing, many substantial farmhouses with orchards,*
> *vineyards and cornfields ... plantations of European trees ... oaks and*
> *poplars he arrived at last at the home of Mr Hart, of Somerset Farm.*

After spending a week with Mr Hart, Pringle and his friend, with their guide, returned home, 'having on this excursion made a circuit of about 170 miles, through one of the best-peopled and wealthiest tracts of our pastoral district'. Mr Hart promised to visit the settlement, which he did shortly after this, and gave the Scottish emigrants much valuable advice. 'The friendship of this able and active man', said Pringle, 'proved indeed both on this and on subsequent occasions, of great advantage to our party.'

Towards the end of March, reassured by the presence of the new guard on the location, Pringle accepted an invitation from Mr Hart to go on an excursion, through a part of the country seldom traversed even by the older colonists. Setting out on 26 March with a Hottentot attendant, they came into the little Fish River area, still suffering from the drought and here saw such numerous herds of springbok, (estimated roughly at not less than 20 000) in view at one time, that 'they literally speckled the face of the country as far as the eye could reach'. These were part of the

---

65. Pringle, Thomas. *Narrative of a Residence in South Africa*, Edward Moxon, London, 1935

great migratory herds of springbok which, during severe drought in their grazing grounds, frequently travelled south into the Colony in search of food, and consumed grazing with the same rapacity and speed as a swarm of locusts.

The country was dry and parched and, apart from the springbok, the only other live creatures they saw were a white vulture, a secretary bird, the paauw, one or two ostriches and numerous lizards.

> *No rain having fallen here for many months, the country was wholly parched up and desolate, and consequently deserted both by the smaller birds and by herbivorous animals. The deep melancholy silence was unbroken save by our own voices and the sound of our horses' feet; even the hum of the wild bees and the chirring of the grasshopper were unheard.*

At sunset, after a tedious and thirsty ride of about fifty miles, during most of which they had seen no sign of water, either a fountain or a pool or stream, they reached the hovel of a Dutch African Boor, situated beside a running stream ,that gushed, cool and limpid, from the savage looking chasm of the Zureberg.[66] Towering behind the poor dwelling were 'precipitous crags which echoed with the barking of twenty or thirty watch dogs and the bleating of sheep'.

The travellers were at once made welcome by the man and his wife. Supper consisted of mutton and potatoes dressed with wild honey; their beds of rush mats stretched on the floor and covered by a blanket of tanned lamb skin with the wool on it. This was generous hospitality from people whose home was merely a sort of wigwam, constructed of a few poles and reeds, and payment was refused for hospitality was never permitted to be paid for with anything other than conversation and, on rare occasions, a gift of ammunition.

The next day they turned southwards, travelling through the Zuurberg

---

66. In current language it is Suurberg in Afrikaans and Zuurberg (pronounced Zooberg) in English

range, intersected by so many deep ravines that they were 'detained and wearied ... exceedingly'. The sour, coarse and wiry grasses growing on the summits had given the name of Zuurberg (sour mountains) to this range and partly accounted for the absence of animals in this area. Further south, in the adjacent plains and valley, where water had collected in fountains and streams, they saw 'several species of beautiful animals ... such as the quagga, the zebra, the hartebeest, rietbok, steenbok, klipspringer, oribi, etc.' and found the rocky ravines inhabited by the dassie (coney) and innumerable baboons.

This could not have been the easiest of journeys, and even less so for a cripple,[67] for Pringle describes the impenetrable vegetation and dangerous rock defiles which, when they left the paths worn by quaggas and antelope, forced them to dismount and drive their horses before them along the precipitous paths. This was the 'foreground of a vast but sombre landscape' which eventually lay stretched before them from the Zureberg down as far as the coastline at the mouth of the Bushman's river. Through the dense jungle they could trace the winding course of the Sundays River, marked by the ,light green willow trees (*Salix mucronata*) growing along its banks. Beyond, far to the south, appeared the Indian Ocean and the shores of Algoa Bay. To the right and west rose the Rietberg Mountains and the fantastic peaks of the Winterhoek. Nearer us, but hidden among the lower hills, and surrounded by dense forests, lay the Moravian Settlement of Enon, which we were in search of. It lay beneath us, for on this side of the Zureberg the low country is much inferior in elevation to the plains on the northern side, and the front of the mountain is proportionately more inspiring'.

This was elephant country and Pringle describes the pathways forced through the bush by 'the monarch and his troop' who, in wearing smooth paths by their habit of always walking in single file and in clearing passages through the dense jungle, performed valuable pioneer services for the

---

67. Pringle sustained an accident in childhood and was obliged to use crutches for the rest of his life

traveller who could not easily blaze such a trail for himself. On their way down and through the bush, they saw many recent signs of elephant and buffalo, and so were not a little anxious to reach Enon before nightfall.

Pringle had already forwarded some parcels of books to the Mission, as well as a letter of introduction from the Rev Mr Latrobe, and was therefore not only heartily welcomed by the missionaries when he arrived, but was pressed to remain with them while Mr Hart went on to Port Elizabeth on official business.

In his *Narrative* Pringle described the luxuriant vegetation and the indigenous forests, chiefly yellow-wood, enriching the valley of the White river (Witte Rivier, a tributary of the Sundays River), with a stately beauty not always met with in South African landscape. He found the cultivation of the Enon Mission inferior to anything he later found at Genadendal, and attributed this to the fact that the missionaries and their flock had only recently returned to Enon after having been forced to flee from the Kaffirs in 1819.

Nevertheless he found the place neat, orderly and demure: 'no noisy activity, but a sort of pastoral quiet seemed to reign through the settlement'. At this time there were three missionaries at Enon, all of

Moravian mission at Enon

them from Germany, two of them plain German mechanics and the superintendent Brother Schmitt, who was married to an Englishwoman, the only white woman in the settlement, 'and exceedingly well-adapted for the station she occupied'.

During the week that Pringle remained at Enon he studied and recorded the flora and fauna of the area, hoped for a sight of elephants and rode about satisfying his enquiring mind on all manner of subjects. Although he did not actually see elephants, he described an incident which occurred a few days before his arrival at the Mission. A troop of elephants had come down one dark and rainy night to the outskirts of the settlement where they were heard bellowing and 'making an extraordinary noise' for a long time at the upper end of the orchard where incidentally, they were in the habit of consuming large quantities of fruit and causing considerable damage by trampling the fences and gardens. No one ventured outside but the following morning the reason for the unusual uproar was discovered. The missionaries had recently dug a six foot trench through the bank of the river in order to lead water on to their garden ground and to drive their corn mill. Into this trench, as yet unfinished and containing no water, one of the elephants had apparently fallen, 'for the marks of his feet were distinctly visible at the bottom as well as the impress of his huge body on its sides'. From the marks found in and around the trench the missionaries concluded that the helpless animal had been lifted out of the trench by the united efforts of his companions who had evidently stationed themselves on either side, some of them kneeling and others on their feet, and hoisted him out.

Before Pringle left he wrote a sonnet on Enon, still greatly treasured at the Mission, and at the end of a week Hart arrived back from Port Elizabeth, and he and Pringle returned home by a different route through the forest. 'The scenery of the Zureberg' according to Pringle, 'far surpassed anything of the kind I had either witnessed elsewhere or formed a conception of from the description of others.'

A few weeks after his interview with Donkin, Pringle went on another expedition on horseback with Hart, visiting all the principal locations of settlers at Grahams Town, Bathurst, Port Frances, Theopolis and Salem. On this trip he was made more aware than ever before of the difficulties of the traveller in this undeveloped part of the Colony. He wrote:

> *In speaking of rivers I may here remark, once and for all, that this appellation is applied by African colonists to every brook that merely exhibits a rill of running water, and even to many that can only occasionally claim that distinction; so that the term often appears, to a European apprehension, very inappropriately employed. The rivers of the Cape Colony, with a few exceptions, are little else than periodical torrents, usually flowing with a diminutive streamlet at the bottom of a huge chasm or glen, the banks of which rise on either hand, steep and shaggy with wood like the side of a mountain; so that in many cases it will take one a full hour to cross from the top of one bank to the other, although the river at the bottom, on ordinary occasions, will scarcely wet your horse's hoofs, as you ford it ... When, however, the river is swollen after rains with a, mighty and furious torrent, it defies all control and obstructs all passage.*

Burghers gathering at Graaff-Reinet

Pringle visited Graaff-Reinet as recorded by Stockenström:

Mr Thomas Pringle, head of the only party of settlers located in my District, reached my house on his way to Cape Town, where he intended to reside, having received from the Governor the offer of the office of Librarian of the Public Library. From what little I knew of Mr. Pringle till then, I entertained a warm liking for his person, and great respect for his character. He was delighted with his then prospects, and happy in the idea that he was leaving his party with the brightest prospects before them, after the arrangements settled with reference to the lands to be granted to them, which arrangements I could point out to him as then in my office, sanctioned by Sir Rufane Donkin the year before. These anticipations, I am glad to say, have been realised to the fullest extent, as the Pringle clan, and their adherents in South Africa, prove and admit, and the old District of Graaff- Reinet may be proud of them, as they ought to be proud of and grateful to it.

To return to Thomas in the Drostdy House, I found him most frank and communicative, very sanguine in his ideas connected with the establishment of a free press in the Colony, and the promotion of education and liberty; and I cannot help thinking that we have been too

SA Commercial Gazette

> *much disposed to overlook the services, struggles, sufferings, sacrifices, and losses, even unto death, of this excellent man in these glorious causes for, among all the compliments which we have been lavishing upon each other, and upon ourselves, his name has hardly ever been heard.*

Pringle took up residence in Cape Town where he opened a school with fellow-Scotsman John Fairbairn who he had befriended while they were both studying at the University of Edinburgh. Fairbairn had not graduated but apparently acquired 'a passing knowledge of classical languages and mathematics'. Instead he became a teacher at Bruce's Academy in Newcastle-upon-Tyne. In 1822 Pringle persuaded him to immigrate to Cape Town, holding out the prospect of a literary and teaching career in the Cape Colony. They launched *The South African Commercial Advertiser* South Africa's first independent newspaper, printed by George Greig, on 7 January 1824. Before then the only news publication that existed was the weekly *Government Gazette*. An article giving details of a libel suit against a Cape solicitor, William Edwards, who had accused the Governor of abuse of his powers, earned the ire of the autocratic Governor, Lord Charles Somerset. Somerset promptly banned the newspaper and decreed that future editions would have to be submitted to censorship before printing and distribution. He also ordered Greig to deposit 10 000 rix dollars with the Fiscal as security in case he should publish anything unacceptable. The authorities' aversion to a free press had been clearly demonstrated some years earlier by the seizure of printing equipment found on board the *Chapman*, an 1820 Settlers ship. In the face of the government pressure, Pringle resigned later in 1824 and left the country to return to Britain. The New Monthly Magazine had published an anti-slavery article which he had written in South Africa before he left. This brought him to the attention of Thomas Fowell Buxton (senior) and Zachary Macaulay which led to his being appointed Secretary of the Anti-Slavery Society.

By the beginning of October 1824 it had become obvious to Thomas that his 'personal prospects in the Colony were for the present entirely blasted' and he decided to return to England where, under the protection of British laws (he would be) 'at liberty to follow whatever course Providence might open ... regardless alike of the favour or the frown of men drest in a little brief authority.'

Leaving John Fairbairn to superintend the remnants of the Academy, which 'now looked like a consumptive patient whose recovery is quite hopeless', and Margaret to look after the house in Cape Town, he set out on a hasty excursion to the eastern frontier. This was the end of the most important phase of his life; never had his hopes and his prospects run so high; never before had they been so utterly destroyed.

Although he was still to write a great deal, and although he was to do a great amount of useful work as a philanthropist, his most creative years were over. Bitterness and cynicism and suspicion had entered his soul. In the ten years of his life left to him he was never again to reach the heights or plummet to the depths he had reached in Cape Town. The letters in existence which he wrote now and until the time of his death give an insight into his character, his aspirations, his principles and his despair, which none of the letters he had written up to this time reveal.

Letters and documents relating to the first twenty years of his life merely record facts; but from the letters he wrote, particularly those he wrote to John Fairbairn during the next ten years, his whole character and personality are revealed to give an almost full picture of the sort of man he was; what he thought, what he hoped for. Had Fairbairn's replies to him been preserved it would no doubt have been possible to judge what sort of a man Fairbairn was, too.

On the face of it, Pringle, disheartened, disillusioned and destitute, left the scene of disaster to try other fields. Fairbairn, less uncompromising than his friend, remained and continued to work under conditions which Pringle considered impossible. When freedom of the press was finally granted to the Colony it was, though inspired by Thomas Pringle, the result of John Fairbairn's untiring efforts.

Back at the Cape, Fairbairn and Greig continued the struggle for press freedom. The newspaper faced further suppression and in 1827 Fairbairn travelled to London to seek justice. The Colonial Secretary gave him permission to re-open the newspaper but laid down the condition that he should steer clear of stirring up and controversy regarding politics. Fairbairn paid scant attention since he now had considerable support from his readers.

Finally in 1829 the press was given absolute freedom from the Governor's control and only three decades later, in 1859, was Fairbairn rewarded for his efforts when parliament passed a bill ending any restrictions on the content of his newspaper. Fairbairn was an old-school liberal who maintained that most conflict on the frontier was entirely the fault of the colonists, not of the Xhosa, and he advocated equal treaties with the Xhosa states based on international law. He was therefore at one with the frontier policy of Andries Stockenström. In 1851 Fairbairn, who was a strong supporter of the multi-racial Cape franchise and the emergent campaign for Responsible Government accompanied Stockenström to London in the hope of persuading Britain to introduce legislation to that effect but it was only two years later, in 1853, that representative government became a reality in the Cape.

The first Prime Minister, John Molteno, hailed Fairbairn as father of representative government and freedom of the press in the Cape. Fairbairn, who had become the sole owner of the Commercial Advertiser when he bought the paper from Greig, enjoyed several decades of media dominance. Things started to go downhill and in July 1853 he oversaw a merger with The Cape Town Mail in partnership with its owner, William Buchanan, the paper being renamed *The Commercial Advertiser and Mail.* When Fairbairn died in 1864 the paper was taken over by John Noble, whose brother Professor Roderick Noble, served as editor but by then Saul Solomon's Cape Argus had made its appearance as a strong competitor. The paper finally shut down permanently in December 1879. Frederick York St Leger[68] was now the dominant media figure with his Cape Times becoming the leading newspaper of the Western Cape.

---

68. The author's great grandfather, founder and first editor of *The Cape Times*

Metrowich's book

13.

Bishop Burnett

Metrowitch[69] writes:

> *Bishop Burnett took passage in the SS Ocean and arrived in Algoa Bay in May, 1820. At the time there was nothing much to distinguish him from the thousands of other British Settlers who took part in the mass emigration. But it was not long before his name became a household word, first in the Eastern Cape, then in the whole of South Africa, and finally throughout Great Britain.*

A fact which forcibly strikes the student of Cape history is the number of violent feuds and bitter public quarrels which periodically broke out between prominent government and military officials in the frontier districts during the Nineteenth Century. It was through his interference in one of these venomous controversies that Bishop Burnett made a violent and dramatic entry into the public life of his new country.

Captain Henry Somerset, in command of the Cape Corps and stationed at Grahamstown, and Captain Andries Stockenström, Landdrost of Graaff-Reinet, had been at loggerheads for some time. Henry Somerset openly coveted Stockenström's position and his friends were actively lobbying on his behalf, suggesting that it would be in his own interest if Stockenström handed in his resignation.

69. *The Valiant But Once*, By FC Metrowich (Howard Timmins (Pty) Ltd

Metrowitch continues:

> *Unfortunately Stockenström had a will of his own and resolutely refused to give up his post. Finding that it was impossible to shift the obdurate landdrost, Somerset's friends changed their tactics and instituted a whispering campaign against him. Certain derogatory stories, which reflected seriously on Stockenström's character and integrity, now began to be spread about the town and Dr Knox, who had formerly been his friend and confidant, was believed to be the chief instigator of these slanderous remarks.*

Stockenström was outraged and demanded a military enquiry but his fellow officers were reluctant to testify on his behalf through fear of offending Governor Lord Charles Somerset.

This is where the controversial Burnett enters the picture. He was an ardent supporter of Stockenström and although it was no concern of his he decided to take the law into his own hands and to become personally responsible for the chastisement of Dr Knox.

> *Armed with a horsewhip he sought out the unfortunate doctor and began to thrash him unmercifully. The latter immediately snatched up his sabre, and tried to defend himself. But although he succeeded in inflicting a slight wound on his assailant, Burnett was too strong for him and gave him a severe beating. Bishop Burnett thus had the satisfaction of giving vent to his feelings. His action, however, was to have dire and lasting consequences on his own life and was in fact to prove the origin of the series of misfortunes and calamities which were to embitter the rest of his stay in South Africa.*

When Burnett first arrived in the Albany District, Captain Somerset had gone out of his way to befriend him, but this savage assault on Dr Knox estranged Somerset, who resented that he had gone over to the other side, so to speak.

Burnett's next encounter was with Robert Hart, from whom he leased a property known as Doon Glen. Burnett had sufficient means at his disposal to farm barley on a large scale to sell to the military establishment in Grahamstown for fodder for their horses. His holdings were extended by a further twelve thousand acres of adjoining land under a grant from Sir Rufane Donkin, the Acting Governor of the Cape.

> *With characteristic energy Burnett set about developing his huge property. He erected houses for himself and his servants, of whom at one time he had nearly sixty in his employ, planted hundreds of fruit trees and acquired a large herd of cattle from Mr. Hart on credit. In fact so lavishly did he spend his money that by the end of the year he found himself in very serious financial straits.*

When Hart demanded payment of the lease Burnett maintained that he was entitled to twelve months credit. Hart threatened legal action against him. Meanwhile Burnett had also run up a debt with a Cape Town firm, Ebden and Eaton, and when this fell due, they demanded a mortgage on his property. Burnett found himself in deep waters. He appealed to the military authorities to pay for the fodder already supplied but this had to be authorised by Captain Somerset and, predictably, no payment was forthcoming. When Hart's legal action came up, the amount was beyond the limit of the Grahamstown landdrost's jurisdiction and it was accordingly transferred to Cape Town. Burnett refused to appear before that court on the grounds that the summons issued to him was in High Dutch which he claimed he could not understand.

> *Robert Hart made the next move. He sought and obtained an ejectment order against Burnett. Three appraisers, one of whom was Pieter Retief, were sent by the government to value the improvements on the estate, and on July 26, a messenger of the court arrived and served a notice on him to vacate his property within twenty-four hours. But Burnett was still full of fight. Not only did he flatly refuse to leave the farm unless he were forcibly ejected, but he also claimed that the valuation put upon his property was*

absurdly low and that Retief and one of the other appraisers were not impartial as they were in debt to Mr. Hart.

Doon Valley was put up for auction and fetched a poor price. Robert Hart, as one of the creditors, was the chief loser and little consolation could be had from the sentencing of Burnett to six months in prison.

Piet Retief
Courtesy Voortrekker Monument Collection

14.

Latter Days

Dutch Reformed Church at Somerset East

The last phase[70] of Hart's long life - he lived to be 90 - was immensely constructive. He had hundreds of friends amongst the Boers, not least Piet Retief,[71] for whom he stood surety in Grahamstown. He probably knew all the leaders of the coming Great Trek. One of his first actions on moving to his own farm was to join with his Afrikaans neighbours in establishing a Dutch Reformed Church as a centre of civilisation and Christianity on the frontier. He held his post as a foundation elder of the Somerset East Church until he was 70 and fought a bonny battle for the Kirk and its independence.

Another of his earliest actions as a free citizen was to found the

70. From: *They Were South Africans* by John Bond

71. Piet Retief was a scoundrel. Were they really friends or simply acquaintances who did some business together? Piet Retief has been venerated through NP/Afrikaner propaganda but for another side of his character, read *Zululand True Stories 1780-1978*, Dr JC van der Walt, Richards Bay Printers, 2007

Agricultural Show of Somerset East - a prodigious novelty on the Cape frontier in 1826. Nominally his friend Landdrost Mackay was president but it is almost certain that Hart was the driving force in this move for better farming.

In his later years the austere, God-fearing old man became a legend on the frontier which he had done as much as any single individual to establish and civilise. One of his descendants, the late Sir James Rose Innes, Chief Justice of the Union, recalled the old man's intense practicableness. When neighbours borrowed his coffin which had been kept ready in the loft according to farming custom, they found Hart had not left it idle. It was packed with dried peaches. He and his son had much trouble to face on 'Glen Avon' as the Colonial wars surged again and again around them. Just after the 1835 war he had 200 cattle stolen and spirited into Kaffirland. Despite his Scottish persistence, even Hart could recover only 23. In the War of the Axe, ten years later, he suffered considerable loss through helping the Government to the best of his powers with cash and grain when everyone else held back.

When the last, worst war of all broke out in 1850, farmers of both language groups in Somerset East felt they could stick it no longer. They met, elected Hart, who was then in his seventies, to the chair, and passed a resolution warning the Government that they would have to trek west to some safer region. Not long afterwards that westward trek began. But Hart himself, our first English-speaking South-African, was made of sterner stuff. Others could trek if they wished.

The old man, a great pioneer, a great farmer and a great gentleman remained to the end of his days in the district which he himself had put upon the map of civilised South Africa.

When the austere, God-fearing laird of 'Glen Avon' passed away in 1867 his tale was not yet done.

Extract from the obituary:[72]

A hearty and most cordial reception awaited any who paid him a visit, rich and poor were greeted with the same welcome, and the number who took advantage of his kindness was not small. His heart was ever ready to sympathize with the needy, and his liberal hand always open to afford succour. None solicited his advice or assistance in vain, and those whom he favoured with either found to their joy, that he was indeed a benefactor. During the Kafir war, Glen Avon was a sanctuary for all, family after family flocked to take shelter under its hospitable roof, and yet although his stores were well taxed and his ingenuity sorely tried to provide for all, none went empty away. When a Dutch congregation was formed, Mr Hart was chosen as one of the Elders of the Church, and to his able assistance and liberality, the present Dutch Reformed Church owes its existence. The Church is also principally indebted to him for the very handsome parsonage which it now possesses. In other matters connected with the progress and future prosperity of the town, the extensive knowledge, ready and valuable advice, and liberal hand of Mr. Hart were freely offered. He continued an elder of the Dutch Church until unable to perform his duties from old age.

Although, in the absence of a Presbyterian Church in the district, Mr Hart joined the Dutch Church, yet he never dismissed from his memory the desire to see a Presbyterian Congregation in the town, but the hand of death visited him ere his desires could be accomplished. Although dead he yet speaketh and a noble monument has he left behind. He has bequeathed £1 300 for the establishment of a Presbyterian cause in town.

The neat little Chapel, at Glen Avon, where the body lay, was crowded, and many could not gain admittance. Addresses were delivered in Dutch and English by the Revds Hofmeyr and Edwards, after which the Pall bearers, Messrs. Hudson, Durandt, Sr., Botha, Schutz, Malan, Pye, Rev. Wither, Frost, Maskew and De Vet, proceeded to their solemn duty, the

---

72. Somerset & Bedford Courant, Sep 21 1867, The late Robert Hart, Senior

procession following slowly and mournfully the mortal remains to its last resting place.

The Eastern Province is peopled with Hart's descendants. Sir Gordon Sprigg, who was four times Prime Minister of the Cape Colony, married one of the grand-daughters of Robert and Hannah and paid a memorable tribute to the patriarch. Sir James Rose Innes, twice a Minister in the old Cape Parliament and eventually Chief Justice of the Union, was a great-grandson of Hart. And in 1937 a great-great-great-grandson, Count Helmuth James von Moltke, came from Germany to visit his mother's native land and his grandparents, Sir James and Lady Rose Innes.

Why mention a passing visit from one who was not even a South African? Because this Count von Moltke[73] paid with his life for those generous and liberal ideals for which, in their best moments, Hart, the first of English-speaking South Africans, and his descendants have stood. Von Moltke could not endure the nation-worshipping National-Socialist system that had gripped his country. In the midst of the Second World War, he struggled with a small group of like-minded men to prepare to save Germany from the political and moral chaos which he foresaw must follow the collapse of the Third Reich. Arrested, then tried for his life by Freisler in January 1945, he was condemned to death. In his last letter to his wife before execution, he wrote in words that Hart would surely have envied: 'Finally I stood before Freisler not as a Protestant, not as a great landowner, not as a noble, not as a Prussian, not as a German even. I stood there as a Christian and nothing else.'

---

73. *They Were South Africans* John Bond, Oxford University Press, 1956

Sir Gordon Sprigg

The Story of Glen Avon

(with acknowledgement to Greg Brown)

Hart Cottage at Glen Avon, circa 1817

Glen Avon is the ancestral home of the Hart and Brown families. It is a place of pilgrimage for other related families wanting to find out more about their roots, be they Pringles, Stretches, Cummings or even descendants of some of the *bywoners* who once lived and worked on Glen Avon.

Glen Avon's spirit is captured in a poem written in 1850 by MB Hudson (Hudson was the author of a detailed work on the country at that time) [74]

The place of Glen Avon, R. Hart Esquire's seat.

Here the beauties of Nature, peculiarly grand,
Encompass a valley where Industry's hand,
Has for many a year with its praiseworthy toil,
Gathered in with rich harvest the fruits of the soil,
To perfection matured by a stream from a fountain,
That in splendour descends from the heights of the mountain,

---

74. Hudson GB, *A feature in South African frontier life, based upon the wanderings of a frontier family, but embracing a complete record of the Kafir war of 1850-51*, Volume 1, J Patterson, 1852

To the purpose of culture subservient made,

By its moisture assisting the plough and the spade.

Here's the orange and grape, with all fruits that we prize,

The gum-tree and cypress that towers to the skies;

Blooming hedgerows of roses the parterres surround,

And the flowrets of England on all sides abound.

By the side of our path as it leads to the hill,

The quince-tree is trained with most exquisite skill,

And a boundary forms to this 'gem of the land'

That must have been touched by some magical wand.

Robert Hart was appointed to take over Somerset Farm in September 1816. He was then living in Grahamstown where he owned property in the town and in the nearby Belmont Valley. He was on a retainer from the British forces and had a young family, and it is assumed he was offered Glen Avon as an incentive to leave a settled lifestyle for a poorly paid job managing the failing Somerset Farm.

Old Homestead circa 1890

What is now known as Hart Cottage, and is run as part of the guest accommodation on Glen Avon, is said to have been built in about 1817. The main homesteads were built (The Old Homestead, 1822 to 1824 and The Retreat, 1824-1826), once official title deeds were received. The deed of grant in favour of Robert Hart, dated 15 October 1821, was for 5 591 morgen (4 790 hectares) in the area known as *Agter op Boschberg*, initially on perpetual quitrent of 112 rix dollars per year, subject to the following; 'to have the boundaries properly traced out and the land brought into such a state of cultivation as it is capable of, within the first three years.' On 8 August 1826 a further 1 852 morgen (1 586 ha) of land adjoining the initial grant was added, subject to the first proviso, but with the following addition; 'That the land hereby granted shall be cultivated by Free Labourers only and that any employment of Slaves upon it shall render the same subject to forfeiture.' This was also subject to an annual payment of 'six pounds six shillings and six pence' to the Receiver of Land Revenues.

The deed of grant in Freehold dated 19 February 1848 in favour of Robert Hart amalgamates four separate title deeds dated between 1821 and 1840 amounting to 16 400 morgen, 'more or less', (14 050 ha) and thereby cancelling the Quitrent.

During the first fifty years of Glen Avon's history, a period in which a number of frontier wars were fought, the homestead served as a refuge to people who had been ousted from areas such as Bedford, Fort Beaufort and Queenstown. Some of the graves in the family cemetery stand testament to this.

Glen Avon Mill circa 1895

The Glen Avon mill is one of the larger of its era in South Africa. It was upgraded to its current state in 1862 most probably by Robert Hart Jnr since his father would have been 85 at the time and can safely be assumed to have retired by that stage of his life. The mill has three floors and is run by a 10 hp overshot steel waterwheel and has French burr stones. It was used in grinding wheat, mealies etc. Installed are a rotary sieve, wheat cleaning machine (smutter), corn crusher, mealie shellers, winnower, bone crusher, saw bench, wood elevator and a wood splitting machine. Farmers came from as far as the Cradock, Cookhouse and Swaershoek districts to make use of the mill.

The crypt or vault as the family call it, is situated in the family cemetery a short walk down Oak Avenue from The Retreat homestead. It is unique in the South African context. It is built into the high river-bank with a façade of excellent stonemasonry resembling church windows, only instead of glass it is slate, on which the inscriptions are carved. There are seven members of the Hart family buried here, the first in 1842 and the last being Robert Hart Snr, in 1867.

The shearing shed on Glen Avon is also of interest to the historian, since it served as the mess hall for the British Army in Middleburg during the Anglo-Boer War. Brown Brothers subsequently bought it and reassembled it for the dual purpose of a citrus-packing shed and a shearing shed. In the 1990's Bill Brown had a modern raised-board shearing system laid out in the shearing shed to improve ergonomics and efficiency.

Some other buildings, as advertised in the sale brochure for Glen Avon in 1937 and which no longer serve their historic purposes, are the shop, dipping tank, cheese house, machinery shed, harness and stabling rooms, cow byre and dairy and meat room. No longer in existence too are the Mill Cottage and cow shed, smithy and piggeries. The dipping tank, built in 1911, by a Mr Bowker[75] is a fine example of stonemasonry

---

75. No doubt a descendant of Miles Bowker, a prominent 1820 Settler

and defines how things were built to last in the 'good old days'.

Robert Hart also built a little chapel on Glen Avon. Many family members were married here over the years and doubtless a few funeral processions will have led from it too. More recently it served as a school for the workers' children. After one of the walls collapsed, the school was relocated and the remaining structure converted and expanded into a tractor garage and goat shed.

Glen Avon is currently a livestock farm with irrigation which augments the livestock enterprise. Currently beef cattle, dual-purpose Dohne Merino sheep[76] and Angora goats are farmed. This however hasn't always been the case. When Robert Hart farmed Glen Avon, the veld was used mainly for sheep farming and the arable land was used for maize, wheat and fruit farming (apple, pear, peach, plum, apricot, walnut and fig). Brown Brothers, who farmed the property from the 1906 until 1937, established it as one of the premier citrus farms in the Union, to the extent that Glen Avon oranges and nartjies were known on the streets of London. Drought, coupled with the introduction of the citrus board (which took over the marketing of all citrus) led to the decline of Glen Avon as a citrus producer. A further setback was an enforced contract to supply the railways in Cookhouse with water for the old steam trains. This fortunately came to an end in the 1980s, after about 90 years of supply, and this enabled Bill Brown to bring irrigation to arable land with efficient gravity-fed irrigation systems. He also stocked the irrigation dams with bass and trout. Glen Avon still criss-crossed with a network of furrows, a reminder of past irrigation methods and some are still in current use.

Professor Robert Wallace travelled the Cape interior in the winter of 1895 and visited Glen Avon.[77]

---

76. A breed of domestic sheep from South Africa

77. Wallace, professor of agriculture and rural economy at the University of Edinburg, was invited by the government of the Cape Colony to investigate its agriculture and farming practices, and arrived in 1895. He travelled all over the colony. The information he collected was written up in the form of a book, *Farming industries of Cape Colony* (London, 1896, 552p), an extensive review, in popular form, of agriculture and animal husbandry in the colony

A few facts relating to the farm of Glen Avon, four miles north of the town, will illustrate some of the chief features of the district. The area of the holding is about 10 000 acres, but only 200 acres are cultivated, and the annual rent is £500. Five years ago, John Cumming, the present occupier, began with 200 cattle, a flock of 1300 sheep, which has decreased to 350, and 400 Angora goats, which have multiplied until they now number 1 100, circumstances which indicate the unsuitability and suitability of existing conditions for different classes of stock. The arable soil is shallow as a rule, and there is a good proportion of heavy clay formed by the disintegration of shale or clay-rock. Mangel wurzel is grown and dibbled out in the field from a seed-bed sown in November.

Robert Hart, in anticipation that a village may develop on Glen Avon, made provision for each of his children to inherit an erf with its own water rights. Glen Avon is no longer in the Hart family since, on 2 July 1867, Robert Hart Junior predeceased his father by a couple of months, during which time Robert Hart Senior did not update his will. After a number of legal opinions were considered, it was decided that Glen Avon would fall in the estate of Robert Jnr and as such, his widow Harriet Elizabeth (nee Marillier) would inherit usufruct of the farm, but not the farm. Ownership of Glen Avon as such was in limbo until she died about 31 years later on 29 August 1898.

Glen Avon was then bought jointly between Hannah Louisa Brown (nee Hart) and John Pringle Cumming (her brother-in-law, married to Sarah Jane, nee Hart). Hannah Louisa became the sole owner on 1 September 1899. Her husband, John Ebenezer Brown was a banker, having come to the Cape from Scotland in 1873, to work for Standard Bank.

John Ebenezer died in 1918 by which time the next generation was already ensconced, farming under the name of Brown Brothers; Lennox, Athol and Colin formed a very industrious partnership, while the purse-strings were still tightly controlled by their mother, Hanna Louisa. This was the era of citrus-farming and capital expenditure. Citrus was planted from 1916 onwards. Lennox was the stockman, Athol the accountant and Colin the nurseryman. 1922 was a significant year, since Brown Brothers installed a private telephone line from Glen Avon to the exchange in Somerset East. In 1925 Hannah Louisa sold Glen Avon to her sons, Brown Brothers, for £25 000. Things must have been very tight, since there was a loan to pay off, citrus had been established and the Great Depression began in 1929. Brown Bros managed to hold things together until 1937, when the ongoing depression (during which for example the price of wool fell 75 per cent), drought and squabbling between the three led to a dissolving of the partnership and Glen Avon being advertised to be sold by public auction on 'Wednesday, 28 April, 1937, 10 a.m.'

For the auction, Glen Avon was split into eight lots, with lots five (Kaffir Kloof) and eight (Irrigation Block) being purchased by Major Pringle from Bedford on behalf of Colin Brown, the youngest of the three brothers. In 1941, Colin bought back most of the original Glen Avon.

Colin Brown's son, Bill was meant to inherit Glen Avon, but sadly he was shot down at El Alamein during World War II and thus his younger brother Bob Brown inherited the farm in 1953. He was determined to restore the veld to a pristine condition, reduced soil erosion work, eradicated harvester termites and cleared invasive 'ouhout' on the mountain. Bob's eldest son Bill farmed Glen Avon from 1983 until 2012, during which time he established modern irrigation systems (the result of the railways water contract being terminated) and improved the veld even further under his curatorship. Since 2012 it has been farmed by Bill's son Greg whose three daughters are the eighth generation on Glen Avon.

For further information on Glen Avon, please visit: www.glenavonfarm.co.za

Appendix One

**Andries Stockenström;
early essay on the wild life in Graaff-Reinet**[78]

The first object that struck me with astonishment was the incredible number of game that literally covered the country. Immediately upon leaving the village, we entered into flocks of countless springbucks, with some half-dozens of ostriches here and there to the foot of the mountain range which constitutes the watershed between the Sundays River, flowing into the Indian Ocean, and the Orange River, which empties itself into the Atlantic.

In the valleys, interspersed among the higher chains of the Sneeuwberg, these animals were found in smaller numbers; but when we descended into the great plains bordering on the Sea Cow River, the endless droves of the same bucks not only, but of wildebeests, quaggas, hartebeests, gemsboks, and blesboks, were indeed astonishing. Lions, of course, were numerous; but we did not see many, and never near; though few nights passed without some damage done by them among the cattle and horses of the farmers at whose residences we were obliged to rest. Since the population has increased, and the springs have been taken possession of, the game and lions have of course greatly diminished, and may in

78. From the Autobiography of the late Sir Andries Stockenström

another half-century become as scarce in the Colesberg district as in those of Swellendam and Stellenbosch. The immigration of the Trek-bokken will, however, for several generations continue periodically to replenish our flats with one species of antelope.

As my first literary attempt, in the year 1824 I sent a brief account of these immigrations to my late excellent friend, the poet, Thomas Pringle, who deemed it worthy of a place in the magazine which he started in Cape Town. He insisted on my trying to contribute, and I wrote to satisfy him, as well as I could, what I feared would not be read; but as it has been translated into several European languages, I need not be ashamed to refer you to it, if you care to know anything more about Trek-bokken and locusts.

Locusts and Trek-bokken

The inhabitants of the Graaff Reinet district have been a good deal alarmed of late by a report that immense swarms of migrating locusts had made their appearance on this side of the Orange River, proceeding southward. From the devastations occasioned by these insects in the eastern parts of the Colony at different periods, there is good ground for those fears if the report be well founded. Since 1808, we believe they have not been seen in Southern Africa but the injury suffered from their visits for several years before that we believe not to be generally known, as we do not recollect to have seen it mentioned by any traveller who has written on this corner of our continent.

From everything we can collect from the most authentic authorities of the Colony, the locusts of Southern Africa are in every respect similar to those appalling multitudes which overran some parts of the south of Europe, and even Hungary and Poland, about the middle of the last century, as detailed in the forty-sixth volume of the transactions of the Royal Society. They have often been seen in such numbers as to obscure the sky where they were passing, and extensive fields in the most promising state of luxuriance have been known to be destroyed and left waste by them in a few hours.

The flying locusts are, however, less dreaded in this Colony than those which have not quite reached that stage of maturity, and are therefore vulgarly called ' voetgangers.'

On the distant approach of the former, if the wind be favourable, by making a fire and causing a dense smoke to overcast the fields, they will generally pass over with the smoke; but the younger or jumping locusts nothing will check in their course, and a powerful stream alone, on the side they approach, can save the crops of the agriculturist from their ravages. Stagnant pools they will cross by the leading multitudes being drowned, and thus forming a bridge for those following; and fires are extinguished by the incalculable numbers, which precipitate themselves on the flames in succession, and by sacrificing themselves provide a safe passage for those that follow.

Their numbers are indeed so inconceivably great that their approach may be justly dreaded; for where there are no cultivated fields to destroy, the pasturage is not a less valuable object to the grazier, who is not seldom driven from the farm those depredators have travelled over to find subsistence for his flocks in those parts which they have missed in their migrations. If they happen to be accompanied, or rather pursued, by the birds called by the African farmer Springhaan-Vogels (as is reported to be the case in the present instance), the prospect is less appalling, as these birds, which seem to vie with the locusts as much in point of numbers (comparatively speaking) as in voraciousness, live on them alone, and consequently soon extirpate them, or at least make them disappear in a short time.

We have not got a good description of the South African Springhaan-Vogel, further than that it is rather larger than the mountain swallow and spotted. They are seldom, or never seen, except when their prey, the locusts, are so very numerous. Not only they, but every animal, domestic and wild, contribute to the destruction of the locust swarms — as the fowl, the sheep, the horse, the dog, the antelope, and everything living may be seen devouring them with equal greediness ; whilst the unfortunate Bosjesmen, and even the less indigent Hottentots, consider them a great luxury, consuming great quantities fresh, and drying abundance for future emergencies. The same is said to be the practice of the Arabs by Drs. Shaw and Russel, and by later travellers in the East, as Burckhardt and others. Great havoc is also committed among the locusts by themselves, for as soon as any one of the number gets hurt, or meets with any other accident which impedes his progress, his fellow - travellers nearest to him immediately turn upon him and devour him with great voracity.

As they are described to do in eastern countries, so also in this, the locusts begin their travels after sunrise and encamp at sunset, and unhappy the farmer on whose fields they happen to quarter themselves for a night's lodgings. When the sun becomes transiently obscured by a passing cloud, they will often stop and collect as if to rest for a night; but as soon as it clears up again they will resume their march or flight. If their halting-place be discovered in the neighbourhood of some farm, the farmer will try to destroy them by driving his flocks of sheep and cattle to the spot before the sun rises to trample them to death; but unless their number be none of the most considerable, little benefit is derived from this effort.

Such phenomena as above described, having been often observed in other countries, will not appear extraordinary in this ; but one, which though not uncommon towards our northern frontier, has not fallen under the notice of those travellers who have published on South Africa (at least, not the notice it deserves), is what our Colonists call 'Trek-bokken.' It is scarcely possible for a person passing over some of the extensive tracts of the interior, and admiring that beautiful antelope, the springbuck, thinly scattered over the plains, bounding in playful ignorance, to figure to himself that these ornaments of the desert can often become as destructive as the locusts we have just described.

The incredible numbers, which sometimes pour in from the north during protracted droughts, distress the farmer as much. Any attempt at numerical computation would be vain, and by trying to come near the truth the author would subject himself, in the eyes of those who have no knowledge of the country, to a suspicion that he was availing himself of a traveller's assumed privilege. Yet it is well known in the interior, that on approach of the Trek-bokken or migrating springbuck, the grazier makes up his mind to look for pasturage for his flocks elsewhere, and considers himself entirely dispossessed of his lands until heavy rains fall. Every attempt to save the cultivated fields, if they be not enclosed by high and thick hedges, proves abortive.

Heaps of dry manure (the fuel of the Sneeuwbergen and other parts) are placed close to each other round the fields, and set on fire in the evening, so as to cause a dense smoke, by which it is hoped the antelopes will be deterred from their inroads. But the dawn of day exposes the inefficiency of the precaution, by showing the lands, which appeared proud of their promising verdure the evening before, covered with thousands, and reaped level with the ground.

Instances have been known of some of these frightful droves passing through flocks of sheep, and numbers of the latter, carried along by the torrent, being lost to their owner, and becoming a prey to the wild beasts. As long as these droughts last, their inroads and depredations continue, and the havoc committed among them is of course great, as they constitute the food of all classes; but no sooner do the rains fall than they disappear, and in a few days become as scarce on the borders as in the more protected districts of the Bruintjes Hoogte and Camdeboo.

The native Colonists themselves can form no conception of the cause of the extraordinary appearance of these animals; and from their not being able to account for it, those who have not been eye-witnesses of these scenes, consider their accounts exaggerated; but a little more minute inspection of the country south of the Orange River solves the difficulty at once. The immense desert tracts between that river and our Colony, westward of the Sea Cow River, destitute of permanent springs, and therefore uninhabitable by human beings for any length of time, are notwithstanding interspersed with stagnant pools, and 'Vleys,' or natural reservoirs of brackish water, which, however bad, satisfies the game.

In these extensive endless plains, the springbucks multiply undisturbed by the hunter (except when an occasional Bosjesman is by starvation driven to make the generally unsuccessful attempt), until the country literally swarms with them, when perhaps one year out of four or five a lasting drought leaves the pools exhausted and parches up the soil, naturally inclined to sterility. Want then, principally of water, drives those myriads of animals either to the Orange River or to the Colony, when they intrude in the manner above described; but when the thunderclouds pour their torrents upon our burnt-up country, reanimating vegetation, and restoring plenty to all graminivorous beings — then, when we could perhaps afford to harbour those unwelcome visitors, their own instinct and our persecutions propel them again to their more sterile, but more peaceful valleys and flats, to recruit the numbers lost during their migration, and to resume their attacks upon us when their wants shall again compel them.

(District of Graaff-Reinet, February 10th, 1824.)

Appendix Two

**Andries Stockenström's views of the Commando System
and the Patrol or Reprisal System**

I must begin with the severely denounced 'Commando System', justly denounced, because it is liable to be grossly abused, as it has been often abused, but essentially and in its origin it is a defensive system, whereas the other system is essentially aggressive. Under the former system the border Colonist was expected and assumed to have his flocks under his eye, and guarded, and he was not allowed to indemnify himself for losses by taking anything from the aggressor. A Commando would consequently never be profitable to him. He had the trouble, the fatigue, the expense, and the danger, but he could bring nothing back except the identical property which had, been taken from him. In defence of his life and goods (unless they could be secured for trial by the legal tribunals), he might even kill the assailants. He might pursue them on the instant alone, or with the help of his neighbours; but he could not continue that pursuit beyond the frontier without the Field-Cornet, or his deputy, who became responsible, and, except in cases of emergency, even that officer required the authority of the Landdrost, who, if there was time, had to apply for the sanction of Government. There was a time when a farmer would have been ashamed to have Kaffir cattle in his herd. They would raise suspicion as to the manner in which they had been obtained, for trade in cattle was not allowed. This was bad political economy, but the object of the prohibition was salutary.

That this system might be and was abused I emphatically repeat. Unnecessary as well as unavoidable bloodshed might take place. It might happen that, if even the stolen property could easily be retaken, blood might be shed from motives of revenge or for the purpose of making prisoners, but this could be checked by having it known as an invariable rule that every collision of the above character becomes immediately the subject of strict judicial investigation, in which such prisoners might be witnesses, so that wanton cruelty was sure to be exposed. It must be remembered that I am not here speaking of Commandos upon a great scale, sent out in times of open war. I allude to the ordinary powers, exercised by the local authorities in case of emergency.

Now take the 'Patrol or Reprisal System'. The farmer misses his cattle; he may honestly believe, or he may pretend that the Kaffirs have taken them, and reports the loss to the nearest military post. The officer in command gives him a patrol, which accompanies him on the 'spoor' which the commander of the patrol, and perhaps he also believes to be, that of the lost or stolen cattle. I have heard it maintained that the farmer is never mistaken on this point, and that an officer, after having been for some time on the frontier, cannot be imposed upon. This I deny. I have passed the greatest part of my life on this service, and cannot trust to my judgment in the matter, and I shall just now give you an instance, of which there have been many, to prove how the most expert spoor-seekers can be deceived. At any rate, a spoor being found, which in a country covered with thousands of cattle is no wonder, it is the spoor of course. Off gallops the plundered owner with the patrol after him, until they pounce upon a kraal, where 'the thieves and liars by nature pretend that they know nothing of any stolen cattle.' The women and children run panic-struck, howling and screaming, into the kloofs and jungles. Compensation having been demanded and refused on the plea of innocence, the patrol collects the cattle belonging to the kraal. Ten fine colonial oxen were stolen, each one of which was worth at least five of these miserable Kaffir beasts, and off away homewards goes the successful patrol and its guide, with fifty or sixty of these beasts, telling the headman of the kraal that he must find the thief, and obtain compensation through his chief. Resistance leads to bloodshed; whether the barbarians thus plundered starve is no business of ours.

But suppose after all this equitable reprisal, or rather, after all this robbery, starvation, and perhaps slaughter, we find on the return of the patrol that the ten fine colonial oxen had, by their owner's neglect, got into the pound, or had been driven by wolves or colonial thieves far in an opposite direction from Kaffirland, or that the claimant for compensation is suspected of never having possessed oxen at all, who indemnifies the kraal, and what do you say of the children that may have perished for want of milk, being too young to seek and live upon wild berries and roots? Or figure to yourself a thief driving the stolen booty by night through, or near a kraal, with the view of misleading the patrol, and then going in a different direction.

The argument is that the men of the kraal can pursue the spoor farther, and will soon overtake the thief. This is very questionable. At any rate, it is monstrously unjust that this kraal should be disturbed at all, and that the whole country should be kept in hot water because I, living near what I am pleased to call thieves and 'liars by nature,' choose to insist upon letting my flocks run unguarded day and night. Besides, even if my ten fine colonial oxen should be found, and the chief should allot them to the kraal which had been plundered by me and my patrol, the very next commando or patrol that should see these oxen in Kaffirland would seize them as stolen from the Colony. In short, there is no end to the evils which this system produces, as the specimen which I promised, and which I now give you, must prove. I give names in order that the official documents may be referred to.

Appendix Three

The Emigrant's Cabin at the Cape

By Thomas Pringle

(1820 Settler - our first celebrity poet, published in 1828)

You'll find, at least, my friend, we do not starve:

There's always mutton, if nought else, to carve;

And even of luxuries we have our share.

But here comes dinner (the best bill of fare),

Drest by that 'Nut-Brown Maiden,' Vytje Vaal.

[To the Hottentot girl] Meid, roep de Juffrouwen naar't middagmaal:

[To F] Which means – 'The ladies in to dinner call'

(Enter Mrs P, and her Sister who welcome their Guest to Africa. The party take their
seats round the table, and conversation proceeds).

P. First, here's our broad-tailed mutton, small and fine.

The dish on which mine diners in ten we dine;

Nezt, roasted springbok, spiced and larded well;

A haunch of hartebeest from Hindhope Fell;

A paauw, which beats your Norfolk turkey hollow;

Korhaan, and Guinea-fowl, and pheasant follow;

Kid carbonadjes, a-la-Hottentot,

Broiled on a forked twig; and, peppered hot

With Chili pods, a dish called Caffer-stew;

Smoked ham of porcupine, and tongue of gnu.

This fine white household bread (of Margaret's baking)

Comes from an oven too of my own making,

Scooped from an anthill. Did I ask before

If you would taste this brawn of forest-boar?

Our fruits, I must confess, make no great show:
Trees, grafts, and layers must have time to grow.
But there's green roasted maize, and pumpkin pie,
And wild asparagus. Or will you try
A slice of water-melon ? — fine for drouth,
Like sugared ices melting in the mouth.
Here too are wild-grapes from our forest-vine.
Not void of flavour, though unfit for wine.
And here comes dried fruit I had quite forgot,

(From fair Glen-Avon, Margaret, is it not)
Figs, almonds, raisins, peaches. Witbooy Swart
Brought this huge sackful from kind Mrs. Hart -
Enough to load a Covent-Garden cart.

But come, let's crown the banquet with some wine.
What will you drink? Champagne? Port? Claret? Stein?
Wel - not to tease you with a thirsty jest,
Lo, there our only vintage stands confest,
In that half-aum upon the spigot-rack.
And, certes, though it keeps the old Kaap smaak
The wine is light and racy; so we learn,
In laughing mood, to call it Cape Sauterne.
  — Let's pledge this cup , to all our friends, Fairbarn!

Bibliography and References

Bond, John, *They Were South Africans*, Oxford University Press, 1956.

Butler, Guy, *The 1820 Settlers – an illustrated commentary*, Human & Rousseau 1974.

Chase, John Centlivres, *Old Times and Odd Corners*, Historical Society of Port Elizabeth and Walmer, 1969.

Cory, George, *The Rise of South Africa: 1820-1834*, Longmans, 1921.

Dugmore, Rev Henry Hare, *The Reminiscences of an Albany Settler, Together with his Recollections of the Kaffir War of 1835*, Grahamstown: Grocott & Sherry, 1958.

Gledhill, Ely & Jack, *In the Steps of Piet Retief*, Human & Rousseau, 1980.

Henning, CG, *Graaff-Reinet: a Cultural History*, TV Bulpin, Cape Town, 1975.

Meiring, Jane, *Thomas Pringle; his life and times*, AA Balkema, Cape Town/ Amsterdam, 1968.

Hudson GB, *A feature in South African frontier life, based upon the wanderings of a frontier family, but embracing a complete record of the Kafir war of 1850-51*, Volume 1, J Patterson, 1852 Jones, E Morse, Roll of the British Settlers in South Africa, A A Balkema, 1971.

Staples, Isaiah, *A Narrative of the Eighth Frontier War of 1851-1853*, The State Library, Pretoria, 1974.

Maclennan, Ben, *A Proper degree of Terror; John Graham and the Cape's Eastern Frontier*, Ravan Press, 1986.

Metrowich, FC, *The Valiant But Once*, Howard Timmins 1974.

Rivett-Carnac, Dorothy, *Thus Came the English in 1820*, Bailey Bros. & Swinfen, 1961.

Theal, George McCall, *Records of the Cape Colony*, Government Printer, 1905.

Theal, George McCall, *History of South Africa from 1795 to 1828*, George Allen & Unwin Ltd, London, 1903.

Tindall, BA, *James Rose-Innes - Chief Justice of South Africa 1914-27*, Oxford University Press, 1949.

Books written, edited and/or published
by David Hilton-Barber

Footprints, on the trail of those who shaped the history of Tzaneen

Footprints, on the trail of those who made history in the Lowveld

Footprints, of those of those who made history in Haenertsburg

Hobson's Choice, Len Hobson, the story of a remarkable man

Triumphs, Trials and Tribulations of a Magistrate in the new South Africa

The Baronet and the Savage King,
the intriguing story of the Tati Concession

The Saint, the Surgeon and the Unsung Botanist,
a tribute to South Africa's early pioneers

Kalahari Dreaming, the romance of the desert

Judge Pat Tebbutt Remembers – a life spiced with variety

The Infamous Malaboch War,
and other gripping stories of the old Transvaal and beyond

The Batubatse, their story and tradition

Salute The Eagle, my experiences as a Parabat in Angola

The Diaries of Sapper Robert Poole

The Lucky Bean Tree,
a hilarious account of a dysfunctional expat family in fictitious Zimbabwe

Matabele Rising, will a two state solution end the conflict in Zimbabwe?

Bitter Aloes, stories of the Eastern Cape